With tl
An intimate guide to

M000031586

Meade Fischer

# Table of Contents

# Introduction

The road sings to me, the hum of tires on pavement, the wind rushing through open windows, the crash of the waves below me, the cries of the sea birds, weaving figure eights in the soft, damp air. It's a song I've memorized over what feels like eons traveling the edge between land and sea, feeling the pull of a long forgotten semi aquatic past, when our almost hairless ancestors, prone to deposits of fat, like seals, made their way through the primal lakes and wetlands of the Rift Valley.

There are moments along this coast that have defined me, like small vials that kept my liquid spirit from pouring away, moments that have come like hummingbirds, a blur, a beating of wings and then the silence of memory. I have gathered my odd pearls of experience on these roads and I've strung them together to create my narrative, and if there are any lessons or bits of wisdom to be found they will be stumbled upon accidentally, the way they have been scattered before me and discovered in my travels.

Chronology is difficult; at least it is for me. It feels as if there is no order to these events, although they did arise in some sequence. It's just that my memory stores according to emotional flavor, rather than in any time order. The order here is geographical.

My intention is to give you an intimate tour of California's central and north coast, to describe these areas in a way that demonstrates their special qualities, to give some information for your travels, and most importantly, to provide a series of road stories that are intended to bring each section of the road to life and to make you feel a part of the area.

But, before I begin this journey, I want to remind you that traveling, like life, needs goals but not a rigid agenda. The best way to travel is to remain open to the experiences that await you, open and willing to pause and savor them. Sometimes you find yourself cramming two days worth of travel into one, and at other times it can take you days to cover 100 miles.

I've tried to write this for you if you are either an adventurer or a casual traveler who has a deep sense of curiosity about

1

anything along the road that looks interesting. So, for the traveler, the families and those without camping gear, I've tried to offer a nice selection of places to stay and to eat, throwing in some bargains with some more upscale places. Even a basic camper like myself gets the urge occasionally for a nice hotel with a warm pool.

If you are a kayaker, this book should be an excellent guide, as I've mentioned just about every good place to launch, some that only a few locals usually know about. For the hiker, I can't promise I've begun to hike all the possible trails on the coast, but the ones I've hiked and loved are mentioned and sometimes even described in detail.

For the camper, I've included state and county parks, BLM campgrounds (my favorites) and even a few places where someone can pull over for the night and "camp" for free.

For the lover of good beer and ale, and I know very few adventure travelers who aren't beer lovers, I've included the wonderful brew pubs along the coast, but just along the coast. For above all this is just about the coast, or, as in some places, as close as one can reasonably get to the coast.

Almost the entire coast is accessible to someone determined enough. You can walk the Lost Coast, along with other stretches that aren't served by roads. However, there are a few places that will get you arrested if you try to explore. Vandenberg AFB is one of these, as is Hollister Ranch at Point Conception. From the south end of Point Conception to Point Sal, there are only two places open to the public. However, if you are a determined surfer and have access to a boat, you can at least enjoy the water off Hollister Ranch, but I wouldn't push my luck with the Air Force, as a military uniform does not mesh easily with the life of an adventurer.

A few tips about traveling the coast include: bring warm clothes, as it can get damn chilly on the north coast, even in mid summer. If you need a nice campground with facilities, such as those offered by the state, make prior reservations, but if you didn't, there are always private campgrounds along the way, never as nice as the public ones, but always with hot water and restrooms. I've included a few of these.

2

Generally, food, lodging and gas is available anywhere. After all, this is the most populous state. However, there are places, such as the Lost Coast, where you can drive nearly a hundred miles without a restaurant or gas station, and I've been careful to note that. I don't want one of my readers calling me from their cell, demanding I come out and bring gas because my book left them stranded.

With an RV or van, you can go anywhere. There are always pullouts and other places where you can simply pull over and spend the night, rarely getting bothered by the authorities, unless you are there multiple nights. With a tent you need to be more prepared.

For detailed descriptions of almost every campground in California, get a copy of Tom Stienstra's *California Camping*. For hiking, Robert Stone puts out a series of day hike books for various locations, covering Ventura through Big Sur. For other areas, stop at local book sellers for titles that cover their part of the state. For kayaking, pick up Michael Jeneid's *Adventure Kayaking Trips from the Russian River to Monterey*. This is a very comprehensive guide to the area, and I am in the process of writing a guide to the rest of the north coast.

I think that the best way to use this book is to read it first to get a feel for the various areas, particularly the ones that sound appealing to you. Then, when you go, take the book along for a mile by mile guide.

4

## Santa Barbara to Morro Bay

To my mind and probably accurate geographically, the central coast starts at Point Conception. That is where a transverse range of mountains, suddenly jutting skyward, cuts off Southern California from the rest of the state, forms the rugged Point Conception area and extends out to sea in the form of the Channel Islands. In other words, I should start this guide at Point Conception, but I'm going to fudge by about 33 miles. On the coast, large cities or towns are often far apart. From Santa Barbara to the next big town, Santa Maria is about 70 miles, another 150 to the next one, Salinas. The bigger towns in between are all under 50,000 people.

Santa Barbara is a good place to start our trip north. It sits just beyond the edge of what we consider Southern California, and it shares a piece of the coast with three excellent state beaches. Also, before going on an extended adventure, it's nice to check into a nice motel, get a good meal, enjoy the last consistently warm beach and perhaps take advantage of nightlife and tourist attractions.

If you get off the 101 at Garden or Castillo Streets, it's a short couple blocks to the **harbor and beach**. There's a pier with restaurants, and at the harbor you can launch your boat, rent one or take a charter. The Maritime Museum is there, along with restaurants and a nice, sheltered beach with volleyball courts, kayak launching and sunbathing. It's a wide beach, in places backed by a wide lawn, and it extends many blocks. Opposite the beach is a row of hotels and motels. The Doubletree resort takes up over a block, and the Best Western sits on the corner of Castillo. There's a

Motel 6 and a Day's Inn near the beach, probably the best bargains within walking distance of the water. However, about a block up Castillo is the Avania Inn, where I last stayed, a bit more than Motel 6 and Day's Inn, but considerably cheaper than the Doubletree. The room had a view of the mountains and was quite large, with comfortable furniture and a rather plush king bed. Best of all, it was quiet at night. There was even a computer with an internet browser in the lobby. There's also the Castillo Inn on Castillo Street and the Hotel Marmonte on East Cabrillo Blvd. off Milpas at the waterfront.

The real gem in the beach area is the Brewhouse. I love brew pubs, and this one had everything going for it. Located at 229 West Montecito, it's walking distance to the beach, has a nice mix of tourists and locals, a great bar, outstanding ales, wonderful food (I recommend the mint lamb burger or the ribs, chased by an IPA), service with a smile and music five night a week. When the **beautiful hostess** welcomes you at the door, you get the feeling you've just stepped into a Bavarian beer garden during Oktoberfest. She exudes the perfect image for her job. I'll never go to Santa Barbara without a stop at the Brewhouse. However, for breakfast along the beach, there's a real blast from the past, the original Sambo's restaurant, from 1957. Contrary to common wisdom, this was actually named for Sam and Bo, the founders. There are tables on the sidewalk, across from the beach.

About four blocks up from the freeway is the historic district, and about four miles from the wharf is the Museum of Natural History and Mission Santa Barbara. A couple miles beyond that is the Botanic Garden. Santa Barbara also has a zoo.

There are many summer activities, including free concerts on Thursday nights from 6-8:30pm, through late August, in Chase Palm Park, at the beach. Dust off your dancing shoes, grab family and friends, pack up a picnic dinner and come on down and celebrate summer.

6

Lower State Street has been converted to a walking mall, with lots of places to eat, drink wine or coffee and go shopping. It is a charming town, full of wealthy people and mostly upscale tourists, but the town also has its poorer, less fancy neighborhoods. Along the beach you can rent bikes and three and four wheel multi-passenger pedal vehicles to ride the bike trail along the beach: 805-966-2282. You can also rent paddleboards and kayaks at the harbor: www.channelislandso.com. Another local outfitter is Truth Aquatics: www.truthaquatics.com. Take a sunset sailing cruise: www.SunsetKidd.com, or beer and wine tours at: www.paradisewineandcitytours.com. Go whale watching with Condor Express: www.condorcruises.com, or sport fishing on the Stardust: www.stardustsportfishing.com. And the one I want to try is Channel Islands National Park sea cave kayaking with Santa Barbara Adventure Company: www.SBAdventureCo.com. They take you out to the islands with kayaks, and you paddle around the sea caves and islands. In short, there's plenty to do in Santa Barbara before you hit the road north.

I take a deep breath when Santa Barbara and UC Santa Barbara at Isla Vista are behind me, along with any rush hour traffic. Soon the road opens up, and it's all rural, and the traffic quickly dies away. Roll down the window, crank up the volume on your favorite tunes, lean back and enjoy. This stretch of road has a special feel for me. Once a Southern California resident, but now, when I have to go back south, perhaps to see an old friend, the press of people and pavement is oppressive, and on that charming slice of road I'm finally able to exhale and substitute daydreams for traffic tension.

There are three state park camping areas and thirty miles of beach between Santa Barbara and Point Conception, all sharing that Riviera climate that makes Santa Barbara such a draw. Unfortunately, people reserve the camp sites, particularly in summer, so getting in is chancy, unless you plan your trips so far in advance that you can pre book. Book today for your grandkids' college graduation. The three are El Capitan, a charming wooded cove, campgrounds among the trees and a long, family friendly beach. It also has some trails that run along a stream, down to the beach and around the campgrounds.

**Refugio** is the next, and it's quite similar to El Capitan. At

the little point, you'll usually see a knot of surfers in the water, waves or not. There is, however, Refugio Road, on the inland side of the highway, which was an adventure on my first visit. It wandered many miles, through the Los Padres National Forest and into the Santa Ynez Valley. Much of it was unpaved, but now the road is closed seven miles in from 101, and there area signs saying no overnight camping. That's unfortunate, as those of us who couldn't get into the campground, would go a mile up the road and camp outside the ranch fences, and it was just as much fun as the state park, because the shared conspiracy of unofficial camping made us all instant friends.

After passing Refugio and before reaching Gaviota State Beach, just before passing a sign that says "Mariposa Reina ¼ mile," there's a wide spot on the beach side, often with cars parked. It's an easy down to a nice, but narrow beach, one that sometimes has nice surf.

Since that particular side trip adventure is off the menu, stay on 101, and the next beach is **Gaviota**, with another campground. Of the three, Gaviota is probably your best shot at finding a campsite, and it is located right where the highway turns inland to Point

Conception. You stand a better chance here because the campground is unappealing, mostly a big dirt parking lot for RVs. However, the beach, which starts under the high railroad bridge, is every bit as nice as any along this stretch.

While you would love to continue along the lovely beach as the railroad track does, the road leading up and north, just before the entrance to the park only goes a short way. While Gaviota State Park extends a bit north, as it does south and east along the 101, most of that wonderful stretch of coast is the Hollister Ranch, being developed for a handful of people who can afford to both enjoy it and enjoy knowing they can keep you and me out.

This is the point where southern California comes to an abrupt end, as the road leaves the beach and heads into a rocky canyon at the southern end of Point Conception. The wind roars up the narrow canyon and almost instantly changes the weather from Riviera to California chilly. There is a state rest stop here, probably the most scenic one in California, so stop, use the bathroom and check out the rock formations above you—something you won't see from the car unless you have a convertible. You can see the jagged sandstone ridges that were once ocean bottom before being thrust up to form that rare transverse range. North of here, the Coast Range, Gabilans and the Sierra Nevada, all run north and south. There's a **rest stop** on either side of the highway, just as

 you leave the coast, and on the southbound side, I've learned that if I'm heading south and pull in and sleep in my van, I hit Los Angeles in the morning, just after

rush hour and can get straight through. There are very few traffic windows in the greater LA area, so you've got to plan.

Exit the rest stop and head through a short tunnel carved out of the rock. You are now in central California, rolling up and over undulating tan hills, studded by oaks, under a soft blue sky.

When you come down the other side of the hill, you hit Buellton, the first town where you can pull off at one exit for food, gas and needed supplies without going more than two blocks from the highway.

Most travelers continue on 101 through Buellton, Los Alamos, and on to Santa Maria, an area that changed a few years ago from ranches to wineries, as in the movie *Sideways*. However, 101 is not the coast, and it's not all that interesting. The better choice is to take Highway One which cuts off a short way past the rest stop. This gives you about 20 miles of uncrowded highway that winds, in long, sweeping turns, through the hills of the east  end of Point Conception. About two thirds of the way to Lompoc, there's the turnoff for **Jalama County Beach**, the only public access along Point Conception, the rest being ranches, such as the private Hollister and Bixby ranches, between Gaviota and Jalama. Above Jalama is Vandenberg Air Force Base, miles of coast off limits to everyone except base personnel. You have to drive 14 scenic, winding miles down to Jalama, which has a campground as well as picnic areas. It also has some serious surf, particularly in winter and spring. It's a good place to pitch your tent for a night or so, away from the mad rush of the highway. As the place becomes more popular, the campground is often full in summer. Day use is $10, tent camping runs from $10-$40, and RV sites with electric hook up are $40. They also have cabins that rent from $80 to $200, depending on cabin, season, weekday or weekend. There's a little stream on the north end of Jalama, and if my memory serves me, on my first visit there was a riparian corridor along there, but it's all open beach now. At that time, I also recall a group of hitch hiking teens camped at the Hwy. One junction. I piled them in my car and hauled them to Jalama. That's another impromptu camping spot that's likely off limits now.

Once back on Highway One, it's a short drive to Lompoc, an unremarkable little town that seems to be rapidly growing, with a few good restaurants, some motels, two little book stores, a quaint old downtown and access to the only other public beach for many miles. Highway 246, which is the road from Lompoc to Buellton, continues on to the west another eight miles to a place called Surf. There's an old railroad station there, and it's actually on Vandenberg land, so the military can arbitrarily decide who uses it and when. What they decided was to close the entire beach during the summer season because of the nesting snowy plover. Now, the plover nests in the dunes, so they could have just fenced those off and left a path down to the stretch of beach everyone uses. Given that people don't walk very far in soft sand, there's little chance of problems more than a couple hundred yards in either direction. However, they chose to close everything from mid spring until the end of summer, which annoys the locals, who have no beach at all.

The upshot is that if you are traveling in what is known as the off season, drive out to the beach and watch the storm-tossed waves beat against miles of deserted sand.

If you plan to stay in Lompoc, there are many nice motels along Highway One. The highway is Ocean as you come into town, and then it turns on H. Street. All the motels are along Ocean/H, and they range from below $100 to just over, making it an affordable stop over. There is also a good selection of restaurants from steakhouses to fast food and even a casino.

Once out of Lompoc and up the long hills, you pass through Vandenberg Village and then the road actually cuts through the base for about fifteen miles. It used to be a two lane road, but it's now mostly freeway. You still don't get the ocean unless you join the Air Force and get yourself stationed there, or until they close it as they did Fort Ord.

At Orcutt, you can take the 135 into Santa Maria and reconnect with the 101, but that's simply boring. Unless you are hungry or tired, there are not many reasons to stop in Santa Maria. Just

11

stay on One which quickly becomes rural again. A short drive past Vandenberg Village, you can turn left on San Antonio Rd. West, for a more scenic route, one that takes you to the village of Casmalia. You'll see Point Sal Road, but that doesn't go to the point. It ends at some ranches, miles from the point. If you continue on and down to the stop sign, turn left. The road isn't marked, but you are back on Highway One. After about 4 or 5 miles you'll come to Brown Road. The sign says **Point Sal** 9 miles. However, the road

washed out in 1998, and it now ends just over three miles in. The road isn't used much these days, and on my last visit a very skinny coyote shared the road with me. The old road wasn't great by any stretch, but it's now more popular as a six mile hike each way, but you only need three miles to view this fascinating point, one that makes a huge "L" shape, the rest of the trail winds down to the beach. Point Sal Beach is just beyond the edge of Vandenberg. There is, however, one other possible way to get there.

About a mile and a half north of Point Sal is the start of the dunes, called Pismo, Oceano, Guadalupe-Nipomo, depending on where you're standing. You can access the dunes and the next actual coastal access from the next town, Guadalupe, a little town with a main street maybe three blocks long, a town that looks like one you'd find in northern Mexico. Half the commercial buildings are empty, and all the restaurants are Mexican except the King Falafel, a place for falafels and burgers.

At the southern end of town, at Main Street, you can turn and go 4.8 miles to Guadalupe Dunes County Park, another coastal access not used by many people. Even though it doesn't cost, there's someone at the gate, handing out literature, apparently to keep people informed about the sensitive bird habitat. Drive through the dunes to the parking lot at the beach, where you can hike beachward of the fence. The rest of the dunes are protected for the terns and plovers. This 18 mile, 22,000 acre stretch of sand dunes extends from Pismo Beach to Point Sal. This particular preserve, with public access, is 592 acres and is available for hiking, surfing, wildlife viewing, photography, fishing and picnicking. It's a fragile ecosystem with endangered species, and 200 species of birds migrate through here. People have been enjoying the area for a long time, perhaps 9000 years, when the first Chumash people settled in the wetlands.

The other way to see Point Sal is to walk a mile down the beach, over Mussel Rock, a 500 foot sand dune, to Paradise Beach and over private land to the point, something you probably don't want to do unless you really love to climb tall dunes.

However, just north along the beach is the wide lagoon that's the **mouth of the Santa Maria River**, a shorter and possibly more interesting walk.

However, before leaving Guadalupe, take a photo, because it still lacks the strip malls and chain stores that typify most other towns.

About three miles north of town there's another intersection, Oso Flaco Lake Road, which leads, in about three miles, quite coincidentally to **Oso Flaco Lake**, which is part of the Oceano Dunes State Vehicular Recreation area. If you don't access the beach anywhere else along here, I encourage you to do it here. For your $5 parking fee you can hike a one-mile trail to the beach. The first quarter mile is on a paved road, under over-hanging trees and brush. Then the trail turns left and becomes a boardwalk over the lake, with views of ducks, cormorants and occasional osprey. On the other end of the lake the boardwalk continues through the thick vegetation of the back dunes, with sage, willow, lupine and other plants, nature's secret garden, nestled among the wide and forbidding dunes. Then the back dunes give way to the more sparsely vegetated mid dunes, before the boardwalk rises to the end at an observation platform above the beach. From there, it's a short walk down the fore dunes to the water. As you walk along, you can see open dunes on the north and south, areas where the dune buggies roam. Also, you can look south to the mouth of the Santa Maria River.

The other way to access this stretch of coast is to head north to Oceano or Grover Beach, at the Pismo Dunes State Vehicular Recreation Area, the dune buggy hub of the coast, enter and drive along the beach, which I believe is firm enough at lower tides for your basic sedan.

Back on Highway One, you soon leave the flatlands and climb gently to the Nipomo Mesa area, heavily wooded with euca-lyptus trees. When it becomes Mesa View Drive, there are some small lakes a block or so west, and west of those are the dunes.

Shortly, the road drops down a long grade into a flat sandy farming area behind the dunes. Unfortunately, there's no good place to pull over to enjoy this startling view.

I have a special memory of this grade. Back when I was a recent transplant to Northern California and still had social roots in the Los Angeles/Orange County metropolis or megaslopolis, I would make several trips south per year to spend a few days with friends. And, since freeways become boring after the second trip, I usually opted for Highway One.

It was early on a spring weekday, so the road wasn't crowded. I had driven through Pismo, Grover Beach and Oceano, in that sandy depression between the Pismo Dunes and Nipomo Mesa, with a stop at the Hayashi fruit stand. So, with a flat of berries on the seat beside me, I started up the grade toward Nipomo.

About half way up I saw a hawk fluttering just above the road. He was obviously excited about something, so I slowed down to see. There in front of me was the biggest gopher snake I'd ever seen. It must have been six or perhaps seven feet long, and it was trying very slowly to cross the road, while the hawk was waiting for me to pass so it could pounce.

It didn't seem right. The road that we built placed an unfair advantage with the hawk. There is no cover for the snake, so it is a sitting duck, or more accurately a sitting snake. I figured the neighborly thing to do was to keep the hawk at bay until the snake crossed the road, thus leveling the playing field. At that point, if the hawk got lucky, it was the natural order of things.

The snake was moving much too slowly for someone being pursued, so I bent down for a closer look, in fact I looked the snake in the eye, a watery, rather dull eye. Then I noticed how it moved, stiffly and with slightly jerky movements. Adding those observations to its incredible size, it struck me that this was one very old snake. The poor thing was arthritic.

Well, my car was blocking the highway, and I stood guard for the longest time until the poor reptile finally made the thick brush on the side of the road. Then I got back in the car and drove off, watching, in my rear view mirror, the hawk fluttering just above the brush, knowing I'd done my good deed for the day and armed with a better attitude toward my destination.

Back on Highway One which turns toward the beach, and at the stop sign at Halcyon, if you really need a town stop, you can turn right to Arroyo Grande. But if you continue on One, you'll see the Hayashi fruit stand on the left. This is one of the best fruit and veggie stands I've ever visited, and they have the best strawberries in the world, bar none. They are the size of small apples, and when you bite into them, the sweet juice squirts down your shirt. Bring a bib and an appetite. You can finish a half a flat before reaching Pismo, 20 minutes ahead. This sandy bottom land is perfect for berries, and I'm thankful that the Hayashi family refused to sell out to the town's development interests.

When you enter the Oceano, Grover Beach area, the road

15

runs along the Pismo Dunes, and there are RV campgrounds, private and state all along the road. If you are buggy about dune buggies, this is the Promised Land, miles of open dunes to roar around.

By the time you enter Pismo Beach, you have a beach town again with a public beach, pier, hot dog stands, beer and suntan lotion, beach chairs, sunglasses, bars, tattoo parlors, lots of restaurants and motels. The center of the community is very much old school beach community, oriented to the tourists who come mainly from the insanely hot central valley to play and cool off for a few days. Since it's the first beach for many miles and close to a major highway, you can realize why it has become a tourist destination.

While downtown Pismo near the pier is very touristy, there is more to the town. The area also has plenty of places to stay in town and also along 101. Just a couple miles south along the 101 in Arroyo Grande, the Best Western Casa Grande Inn, at 850 Oak Park Blvd. has lovely grounds, a nice looking building, comfortable beds and a pool, and the prices are very reasonable. It's also up on the hill, so if you have a west facing room, you have a view. Call 866-539-0036. This is one exit south of central Pismo. Also, there's a new Hampton Inn that also faces Pismo from up on the hill.

I go into Pismo, sample the atmosphere, maybe grab a sandwich and a beer, but I don't hang around. It's not for the adventure traveler. A mile up the road is Shell Beach. Head north on Hwy. One, but don't get on the freeway (101). Instead stay on Price Street, which turns into Shell Beach Road, which follows the freeway.

Keep driving a few blocks to the corner of Shell Beach Road. and Cuyama Avenue. Central Coast Kayaks (805-773-3500, www.centralcoastkayaks.com) has rentals and tours. If you have

16

your own boat, drive down **Cuyama to the beach** and look around for the steps down to the beach and reef. In summer you can launch and   paddle among the rocks. If you don't like the idea of carrying a kayak up and down stairs, bring a 20 foot piece of rope and lower and raise it from the top. Central Coast can also take you a bit further up the road to Avila Beach, another easy launch, where there are some fun little sea caves and an interesting shoreline to discover. Avila is semi protected by the breakwater at the end of the point, which creates the Port of San Luis. The port is home to commercial and recreational craft, and it's a large port. Avila also has a flea market on Friday afternoons, making parking a bit of a problem.

If you are driving to Avila, stay on Shell Beach Drive until you come to Avila Beach Dr. and turn left, winding your way down to the beach. Note that you can park and **launch along the road**, and there's a real port at the end of the road. Paddling in the harbor is pleasant because it is protected, but go around the break-water and you get slapped by the wind. And, if you take a tour with Central Coast, you'll probably be hungry when you get back to their store, so just down the street is Mei's Chinese Restaurant, a popular place with locals.

Once you leave Avila, you have to either get back on the 101 or take a long, wandering adventure through See Canyon. As you drive back toward 101, take a left on San Luis Bay Dr., and a bit further, another left on See Canyon. San Luis Bay is also an exit from 101. On this route you can cover what takes 10 to 15 minutes on the highway in under two hours, but what a fun two hours. This winding canyon road meanders through the hills, passing lots of apple places, some with stands where you can pick up bottles of apple juice and cider, maybe even hard cider. About three miles in is a fairly new place, **Gopher Glen**. They have apple tasting, fruit, fudge and other goodies. They are friendly folks, and they stay open until 5:00.

About a mile up See Canyon is Kelsey See Canyon Winery. The have a zinfandel that they are pretty proud of, and it was on sale on my last visit: http://www.kelsey-wine.com/.

See Canyon is a narrow, rural road, and when you get to the top of the canyon, about 10 miles, you intersect with Prefumo Canyon Road, a one-lane dirt road that heads off to the right, steeply down, eventually winding its way to Los Osos Valley Road. From there it's just a few blocks (right turn) to the freeway. This is not a road for the faint of heart. It even makes some of the locals nervous, but what a view from the top!

From Los Osos Valley Road, you can choose to go left, through Los Osos and on to Montana De Oro State Park. The park has campsites and some cove beaches that are very popular in the summer. There are also a number of hiking trails, and one up to Va-

lencia Peak isn't terribly long, but affords a sweeping view from the top. You can also launch a kayak from some of the coves and explore this wild section of coast. The area between Port of San Luis and Montana De Oro can't be driven, and the **Diablo Canyon Nuclear power plant** is right in the middle, and that's definitely not open to the public. However, you can hike part way. Drive to the end of Montana de Oro and park in the last lot. Walk through the gate, over Coon Creek Bridge to the PG&E

check-in station. You must register and stay on the trial, which passes through a working ranch. The Point Buchon Trail, open Thurs. through Mon., follows 3.4 miles of magnificent coastal bluffs. Windy Point, at 2.6 miles, affords a view of the Diablo Canyon plant, looking like a gray, Turkish temple in the distance. This is not to be missed.

But, it's late, and you don't want to go back to stay in Arroyo Grande or Pismo, and you are in Los Osos. You can take Bay Blvd. through Baywood Park and over to Morro Bay and save the long drive through San Luis Obispo and back to the coast.

However, if you do drive back to the 101, on the next exit, Madonna Road, is the famous Madonna Inn, right off the freeway. They have regular rooms and theme rooms, such as "caveman," "Daisy Mae," "Captain's Bridge" and "Buffalo Room", and the whole interior is so ornate and fun to wander through. Even the men's restroom off the lobby is a work of art, with the giant sea shell urinal. Stop, walk around, grab a bite, and if you feeling like splurging, spend the night. They have their own bike trail, three quarters of a mile, which connects with Marsh Street in downtown San Luis Obispo, saving you from getting on a busy road. From town you can connect to an open space for a bit of mountain biking.

If you are on a budget, there are a host of motels in San Luis Obispo, just a couple miles further. Many of these are on Broad Street. And, if you are spending the night and don't have to drive, you have two brew pubs to enjoy. Creekside Brewing Company, with hand-crafted ales, pub-style comfort food, scenic patio dining, local wines and full bar, is at 1040 Broad Street (805) 542-9804-www.creeksidebrewing.com. Downtown Brew at 1119 Garden St. (805) 543-1843 www.dtbrew.com is another place to enjoy some micro brew.

From San Luis Obispo, people in a hurry to avoid fun and beauty jump back on the 101 and head toward Salinas. You, being an adventurer and not in a big hurry, will take the Highway One exit and drive the fifteen miles to Morro Bay, past the great rock peaks left over from ancient volcanic days. Then you'll be poised to enjoy the scenic San Luis Obispo north coast and Big Sur.

If you end up heading over to Morro Bay, the Inn at Morro

Bay's Cape Cod-style buildings overlook picturesque Morro Bay, with 4,000-acre Morro Bay State Park as a backdrop. From the Inn, you have the state park, the bay and a golf course right at your fingertips. It's a good place to stay in Morro Bay. Just up the street, Morro Bay Sandpiper Inn is a short walk to the Embarcadero, and when not busy, you can negotiate the room rate. Also, check out the La Serena Inn.

If you are like me and would rather camp and save your money for good food and beer, Montana De Oro State Park has camping, and I don't know how crowded it is, so check with them before going. Also, you can drive seven miles up Hwy. 41 at the north end of town to a lovely BLM campground, in a shaded canyon.

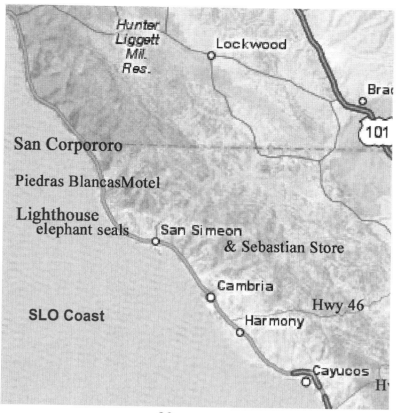

# San Luis Obispo North Coast

You've arrived at **Morro Bay** either directly through San Luis Obispo or in a delightfully slow meander over See Canyon, through Los Osos and Baywood Park. And if you are not camping you've spent the night in town. Now you are ready to explore a very special slice of the coast, one that gives the illusion of being semi deserted, even when the tourists are out in force.

While most of Big Sur seems to hang from high cliffs, cut by deep, forested canyons, the San Luis Obispo coast is gentler, more rolling, with coastal terraces and small drops to rocky beaches. Once north of San Simeon, it's open road, except for the few luxury homes being built on Hearst Ranch, and the Piedras Blancas Motel which sits alone, forlorn and isolated. Most of this coast appears deserted, but eventually beach lovers will discover the hidden charms of the open beaches and secluded coves now under public ownership.

Morro Bay has grown, and now it almost reaches up the coast to Cayucos. Morro Strand is that long stretch of open beach, fronted by new housing developments, that reaches north from town. However, the town itself is worth exploring. Famous for the rock, a 581-foot volcanic plug that guards the entrance to the harbor. And no, you are not allowed to climb it, but you can drive half way around it.

21

On the landward side of the rock is a huge dirt parking area for the beach, which is a great surfing, sunning and bathing beach, under the shadow of the rock. And on the opposite side is the entrance to Morro Bay, stretching five miles south, paralleling the ocean and reaching all the way back to Los Osos/Baywood Park.

Before exploring Morro Bay, let's make a quick trip back to Los Osos, via So. Bay Blvd, reached by continuing south on Main through the state park. Between So. Bay Blvd. and the back of the bay you'll find the **Elfin Forest Preserve.** Turn right on Santa Ysabel Ave, off So. Bay, and right on any of the next few streets to park and walk the approximately one mile loop, mostly on a boardwalk. Along with great views of the bay, rock and surrounding hills, you'll see a rich selection of coastal shrubs, along with a small forest of trees just tall enough to walk under. It's ten minutes from downtown Morro Bay, and you can walk the loop in about a half hour, coming away with a real feel for this coastal, back-bay environment.

Back in town, you can **rent kayaks** down on the Embarcadero and spend several leisurely

hours exploring the bay. You can even paddle over to the strand

and walk over to the ocean, where you will have almost five miles of beach mostly to yourself.

To get down to the Embarcadero, take the Main Street exit when coming from the north or the Morro Bay Blvd. exit when coming from the south. Morro Bay Blvd. will drop you down to the docks, where you'll find several places to eat overlooking the bay and the rock. Windows on the Water, Restaurant & Bar, Flying Dutchman, Rose's Landing, Tognazzini's Dockside, Outrigger and The Galley are all located on the Embarcadero, and once parked, you can walk to all of them.

While in town, stop at Coalesce Bookstore at 845 Main Street, just off Morro Bay Blvd. This is one of my top ten independent bookstores on the West Coast. Pick up a book, and tell them I sent you. They also have a wedding chapel in the back, in a lovely setting.

Once you head north out of Morro Bay there are few routes back to the 101 freeway. Highway 41 is on the north end of town. Highway 46, just south of Cambria, goes over the hill to Paso Robles. Nacimiento Fergusson Road at approximately Monterey's milepost 19, opposite the Kirk Creek campground is the next through road, a winding, seemingly endless, but lovely road that takes you through Fort Hunter Liggett and eventually out to King City. There's not another road heading east for over fifty miles, at Carmel Valley Road. In short, you've got three chances to change your mind, but who on Earth would want to leave this most beautiful meeting of land and sea?

Assuming you are committed to 100 plus miles of scenic coast, continue just a short way north, and you run into Cayucos. This is a small beach town. The downtown is quaint, with some old fashioned buildings, some surf shops, snack bars and restaurants, stores and bars. There's even a new winery downtown with excellent wines. It was in Cayucos, years ago, at a little bar and grill, that I first tried microbrew ale, which turned me from a beer drinker to an ale aficionado. It was an impulse order, and after one sip, I was transformed, and it was only Sam Adams, the "gateway drug" to really fine microbrews.

Cayucos is a beach town, complete with a pier, long sandy beach and fun little surf. Again, it's a great place for people from the hot Central Valley to come to cool off for a couple of days and play in the ocean.

Just north of town you'll find a very wide dirt area stretching along the ocean side of the road, big enough for dozens of cars. Stop. On this stretch of highway, you simply can't be in so much of a hurry that you can't take one of the dirt trails down to the bluff to see the rock-strewn little coves. You can choose a trail down to the rocky little beaches and have a piece of the coast to yourself.

Driving north from Cayucos, you will pass the Hwy. 46 cut off, the 20 some mile route back to Paso Robles, and a wealth of wineries. Yes, Paso wines are every bit as good as those in Napa.

Just a couple miles south of the Highway 46 junction is the town, and I use the term loosely, of Harmony, population 18. Just off the highway, Harmony sports an old building that used to have several shops and the post office. Not sure if any of those shops are still open, but off to one side and behind is a pottery shop with many distinctive plates, cups, goblets and anything else you can make out of clay. They make them and sell them there. Up the hill from that is the winery, Harmony Cellars. I'm no wine expert, but if I find their wines good, the winery atmosphere makes the wines seem even better. The only other structure is at the end of the one street, a glass blowing studio that has had many incarnations in the years I've been visiting. Depending on which glass blowers are in residence, the work ranges from awesome to mind blowing. You simply cannot come this way without stopping.

From Harmony, you drive through wooded hills to Cambria. As you approach it from either direction, there is a turn off on the  ocean side for **Moonstone Beach**. A road runs for about a mile along the bluffs, above a dark sand beach that just begs to be walked along. On the other side of the road is a row of motel/lodges, a couple of art galleries and the occasional place to eat. Moonstone is the consummate romantic weekend getaway. The whole place has a honeymoon or anniversary feel to it. It is also one of the best surf beaches in North San Luis Obispo County. I tend to be a camper, so I haven't stayed in any of these places, but they all look charming and you can check them out on line at: http://www.cambriachamber.org/motels-beach.php.

There is a signal on the south end of Moonstone Beach, with the main part of Cambria on the inland side. This is the last

signal heading north until Rio Road in Carmel, a hundred miles away. It's the place where the traveler lets out a long sigh before hitting the gas. **There's also has a launch ramp** for your kayak.

Cambria has some nice little eateries along Main Street, along with some art galleries, Artifacts Gallery, being one of the most interesting. Bill La Brie's incredible photo gallery, Visions of Nature, is across the street from the gallery, both in the 700 block. There's also candy, ice cream and coffee stores and more places to stay. It's the last tourist kind of town for many miles and a popular destination for weekenders. There are the west and east villages, with about a half mile in between. There are a couple of winery tasting rooms in west village for lovers of the grape. My favorite is the very casual and friendly Moonstone Cellars Tasting Room at 801 Main St. # C. The Vault in east village is a place to stop for both art and exceptional art glass. The Bluebird Inn at 1880 Main Street is the largest motel in east village, and it's a very comfortable place.

For the camper, go a couple miles north to San Simeon State Park. State park rates are not stable, due to California's financial problems, so it's hard to say what a camp-site will cost. The camp-ground is, however, across the road from the beach.

**San Simeon** is about 4 miles north of Cambria. There are a few small stores, Friends of the Elephant Seals headquarters and several motels and places to eat. The San Simeon Lodge serves a very good breakfast, and I assume lunch and dinner are equally good. I don't know about the accom-modations, but the place looks nice and is well kept. On the other side of the highway and on the south end of town is the Sea Breeze Motel that advertises all non smoking rooms, a big plus these days, and some of them have an ocean view. Recently I enjoyed a special at the Quality Inn, offering a package of two nights, tickets for Hearst Castle, breakfasts and one dinner, and they have a very nice restaurant. The rates were very reasonable. There was a bit of an ocean view from our room, and after a rain that first afternoon, we enjoyed a rainbow from the balcony. Also, on the northeast end of town, there's a convenience and liquor store, where you can pick up snacks, a six pack or a bottle of good wine.

Less than two miles from the town of San Simeon is I guess what you'd call old San Simeon. It's where Hearst Castle is, along with W.R. Hearst State Beach, the historic **Sebastian Store** and the original old school house (M.P. 57.8).

You can turn right to the castle parking area, get tickets to one of several tours, see the great short film on the history of the

26

place, grab a snack and buy clothing and gifts. You can also turn left to the state beach, which has free parking, a fishing pier and a calm beach backed by the three mile headland that juts out and hooks slightly south. There is a kayak rental outfit there, but it's hard to say when they're open, probably on weekends. The Monterey Bay National Marine Sanctuary has a visitor center there, in a trailer.

This is a great place for a short kayak trip, along the headlands and out to the point and beyond when the wind isn't blowing. I've **paddled among dolphins** out there, and there are always flocks of sea birds. The beach is very family friendly and the one place crowds gather on sunny days.

The Sebastian Store, across the road from the beach, is the last business in the San Simeon area, and the last for about 20 miles. It's on the left side of the highway, opposite the entrance to Hearst Castle and on the road that leads to the state beach. While it's been in the same family since 1814, the new management has fancied it up a bit, and you can get a good lunch to enjoy on their deck and taste some quality wines at their wine tasting bar. Since it's a general store, there is a good selection of things a tourist might wish to hAvenue

From the parking lot, look inland at the original one room school house, left over from the days when this coast was truly isolated. Hearst Castle stands out along the ridge behind the old school, a true photo opportunity.

One popular spot just north of San Simeon is Arroyo Laguna. There is room for maybe a dozen cars, and a metal gate leads to a short sand path to the beach. Surfers and beach lovers have hopped the gate for years, but now there is pedestrian access, making it even more popular. On a recent visit, with the afternoon wind

**Arroyo Laguna**

blowing, I found a large contingent of kite surfers in the water and on the beach, while a solitary surfer tried to grab a last few waves before the wind trashed the surf.

Over the years, people have backed campers up to the fence at night, and some have carried their tents over the metal gate and down to the beach. Now that it's a public beach, time will tell how well the public cares for it. Sometimes the elephant seals invade this spot, and you walk right by them on the way to the beach.

That small parking area is one of the few places left along that stretch that doesn't sport a sign prohibiting camping, so I usually spend the night backed up to the fence, enjoying the solitude, sleeping like a baby.

The rest of this coast is free and open, with sweeping vistas. The only structures on the coast side south of Big Sur are the Piedras Blancas Motel and the lighthouse. A couple of years back I stopped at the motel, which has been closed for some time, and Tamara, the local ranger was repainting the interior. I don't think there is room in the state budget for an assistant, so who knows how long it will be before the place, now state property, will reopen.

From San Simeon to San Carpoforo Creek, some 18 miles, you have new state land to enjoy. Once part of the Hearst Ranch, the state bought the strip between the highway and the ocean around 2005. It is public land now, but it isn't what the public thinks of as public land. There are few signs indicating public ownership, no restrooms, picnic benches or toll booths. There are a couple of paved scenic area parking places, including the busy, elephant seal viewing spot just south of the Piedras Blancas Light house (M.P. 65.1). When the **elephant seals** took over the beach in the mid to late 90s, this little used beach suddenly became popular.

A parking lot was installed and parking along the highway was prohibited to ease the congestion caused by hundreds of people stopping to watch these massive animals. Except for this elephant seal viewing area, the state's low profile allows the best of two worlds, public access without overuse.

Changes along the scenic north San Luis Obispo county coast are gradual and subtle. To the casual tourist passing between Hearst Castle and Big Sur, this windswept and seemingly wild stretch from San Simeon to San Carpoforo beach looks much like it did when it was still part of the Hearst Ranch and nominally closed to the public. A fence still runs along the west side of Highway One, and the coastal bluffs are still mostly deserted, undeveloped and crossed by old foot paths created by generations of fence-hopping hikers, surfers and beach lovers

For those of us who have wandered the old trails down to the beach for years, certain changes are obvious. There are several **access gates or stiles**, V shaped wooden entrances that allow foot traffic but discourage bikes and animals. Tamara, the "lone" ranger for the area, has also built these several entrances, as well as posting the few signs along the road. But, be warned, nothing here is obvious, and you must keep your eyes open.

Most travelers are, like I still am after countless trips, bewitched by the sight of miles of open coastal land, or as the Coastal Commission staff report put it: "An unspoiled shoreline with hundreds of coves, dozens of uncrowded beaches, rocky headlands and clean blue water stretching to a far horizon unmarred by oil rigs or air pollution, one of California's premier wonders." On the east, there is minimal development on the ranch, and to the west is a seemingly wild stretch of rocky coast with almost hidden little beaches. To drift lazily over the undulating road is mesmerizing, creating the feeling of falling back in time to the turn of the twentieth century. After a few minutes the scenery diffuses almost into a daydream, and the driver may not even notice the odd trail heading to the water.

About three miles north of San Simeon and Hearst Castle, the **Piedras Blancas Light** sits out on a promontory. Just before the lighthouse, there's the parking lot for elephant seal viewing, usually crowded when the seals are active. The viewing area takes you very close to the animals, and you don't have to walk too far, and it's always worth taking a few minutes to stop and perhaps take a photo.

Before the elephant seals took over, the road moved and parking along the low bluff forbidden, one could pull off and park, even spend the night, as I've done several times. Tiny waves wrap around the lighthouse and collapse on the gravel beach. The most memorable of these nights was during early March in one of our El Nino years. Every creek in Big Sur was overflowing, creating waterfalls over fallen trees. As night was falling I pulled off along the bluff and crawled into the shell of the little pick up truck I had. While I sipped wine and read my book by the light of my battery powered lantern, the storm outside rocked the little truck, and great gushes of rain beat on the sliding windows. I was surprised the old shell didn't leak. Between sheets of rain, I saw the light flash as it came around every few seconds. I fell asleep to the sound of rain and wind, and when I awoke in the predawn hours, the sky was clear, the wind calm and everything seemed surreal, like a still photograph, with the small waves lapping the shore the only things moving.

One day I pulled up and stopped to take in the view of the two little rock islands a half mile from shore. They looked like two lonely sentinels or two lovers not quite able to touch. The scene was just too perfect, the water intensely blue, the sky dotted with puffy white clouds. I pulled my kayak off the car, dragged it down the bluff and paddled out, going around the bigger island, where hundreds of birds were nesting, riding the surge between them, and making again for the beach and my car, seeming quite small and remote, alone on the road.

Piedras Blancas Light Station itself is open for tours. Tours are offered September 1 through June 14 on Tuesday, Thursday, and Saturday at 10 a.m. From June 15 through August 31 tours are offered Monday to Saturday at 10 a.m. Tours last two hours and include the historic lighthouse, support buildings, wildlife viewing and spectacular scenery along an easy ½ mile interpretive trail. Dress warmly, but don't bring your pets. Meet at the former **Piedras Blancas**

**Motel**, located 1.5 miles north of the light station at 9:45 a.m. Do not wait at the gate to the lighthouse! The price is $10 for adults, $5 for ages 6 -17, with no fee for children 5 and under.

I'm hoping that the state will finish remodeling the motel and open it up again. It's out there by itself, along the bluff, a perfect place for getting away from the hectic city.

Another wild and rugged beach is accessible, just north of Piedras Blancas lighthouse. There is room for three or four cars to pullout on either side of the road, and it's no longer necessary to climb over a barbed wire fence to reach the beach, long a popular surfing area. This beach, facing north, has the most impressive surf, and, as I saw recently, attracts couples who want a solitary place to picnic. A foot path leads down to and along the bluffs, and there are some visitor-made trails down to the beach.

While the beach is often only a few dozen yards from the highway, in places, such as Arroyo De La Cruz about two miles north of Piedras Blancas, there is almost a mile of riparian corridor from the highway to the mouth of the year-round creek, A trail drops down from the north side of the bridge, with one fork to the creek, the other along the riparian corridor. Another access to the creek is about a five minute walk. Beyond that the trail eventually loses itself in the thickets of brush, so if you want to get to the beach, put on river sandals and walk down the creek. On my last visit I saw a coyote, fattened up on all the cottontails in the fields.

There are a couple more places with those V shaped gates, no sign, and just a trail off into the brush. There are no destinations here. One just walks along the bluffs, among the wildflowers, avoiding the poison oak, and down to the beach.

A bit south of San Carpoforo there is a trail through an opening in the fence at Arroyo Hondo at Breaker Point. It isn't something newly built by Tamara, not a stile, but a hard to notice trail that leads through trees, shrubs, poison oak and ice plant to a cove reminiscent of the Mendocino Coast. Rugged rock formations jut from the shallow cove, and the place would invite kayaking, if it weren't for a difficult, fairly long and narrow trail. While only ten or fifteen minutes from road to water's edge, it's a long way to carry a 40 or 50 pound kayak. It is a great place for beach combing and picnicking, and you have a better than even chance of having it all to yourself.

Where this coast ends and Big Sur starts is marked clearly at San Carpoforo Creek and Beach. Once private with the only access being from a trail down the bluff at the south end, it is now public beach, with room to park two or three cars across from the house that sits above the creek and across the highway in front of the beach. A dirt road runs uphill next to the house, climbing steadily above Hearst Ranch and back into the Silver Peak Wilderness. One can throw on a backpack and wander for days, coming down at any of a dozen trails back to Highway One. If you go down to the beach, stay on the path until you hit the actual beach.

One reason they don't advertise access here is that it is breeding ground for endangered birds. It's an amazingly natural place, so treat it with love and care.

What always moves me is the **approach to San Carpoforo from the south.** Highway One undulates along this sweeping, rolling ranch land and then up ahead the vertical escarpments of Big Sur suddenly jut almost straight up. It's so sudden that it seems like the land ahead was violently bent ninety degrees by some massive, unseen hand.

First the road drops to **San Carpoforo Beach** and then climbs steeply hundreds of feet in less than a mile. And then you find yourself in Big Sur, a different place, a different mood, a different life style. While still in San Luis Obispo County for a few miles,

33

even a bit past Ragged Point (M.P.72.9), this sudden climb marks the edge of Big Sur.

There's always a subtle mood shift that comes over me as I drop down from the bluff to San Carpoforo Creek and start the steep climb to the winding, cliff-hugging road that clings to the Big Sur coast. But one can't just be dropped into Big Sur. It must be approached. Let's approach it from the south.

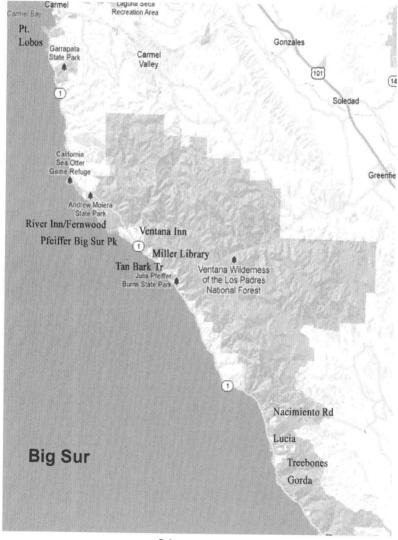

## Big Sur

Long before I moved north, when I first started traveling out of southern California, I had two interesting experiences, both near the Monterey/San Luis Obispo County lines in southern Big Sur, somewhere between San Simeon and Gorda, although at the time neither of those names meant anything to me. I don't remember which came first, so this is either a story of karma or paying it forward.

A car was pulled over along the side of the road, the sun starting to set over the ocean. Two young women were having car trouble, so I stopped. With the rugged cliffs ahead, I figured that there would be no services up ahead for many miles, but I recalled something further back, perhaps either San Simeon or Cambria. Even though I was trying to get to San Francisco that night, and night was fast approaching, I drove them back, but I don't remember if I left them with a mechanic or picked up what they needed and returned them to their car. I know a considerable amount of time was lost from my schedule.

The other event, a year or so before or after, was along the same stretch. This time it was me with the car problem. I had one of those old VW bugs that was always breaking down but was easy to repair. I shifted and nothing happened, so I coasted over to the side. Following the sounds, I pulled out the back seat and discovered the box where the shift linkage from the gear shifter connected to the transmission. The pin in the linkage had broken. A car pulled up, and a couple on vacation asked if they could help. I noticed they had something interesting, a pole that connected to the two clothes hooks above the two back doors, turning the back seat into a closet for hanging garments.

I looked at that and back at my unlinked linkage and got an idea. "Can you spare a wire coat hanger?" A few minutes with a pair of pliers, and I'd wired the linkage back together. Sure it wasn't tight, and the shifting was sloppy, but it shifted, and as I recall, I don't believe I ever had it fixed properly, leaving it that way until I sold the car.

Since then, that has always been a special section of the coast for me, and over the years, many delights have come my way along that stretch, a place I often camp alone, reflecting in silence on the utter peace I always find there.

There are places along the coast where one could easily spend a full day, a weekend or even a week. Big Sur is a place where you can spend eternity and still think the trip was too short. A case in point was Lucy.

A few years back, I saw a notice at the River Inn in the heart of the Big Sur valley. It said that a poetry group meets in the lobby of the restaurant on Tuesday nights, so I thought, Big Sur and poetry, why not. Lucy was the informal leader of the group, and everyone read from their favorite poets or even their own work.

At the time Lucy was in her late 60s, a total bundle of energy with an animated face. In time I got to know a bit about her. Apparently fifteen years earlier she had taken a west coast vacation on a tour bus. She'd lived and worked in New York City. The bus cruised down from Monterey, stopping for lunch at the River Inn. Lucy got out, looked around, went back to the driver and asked for her luggage. "This is as far as I go," She said, and she'd been there ever since, going back for a week each summer to visit her kids. She worked part time as a hostess at the River Inn, and she lived up on the ridge in a cabin with no electricity, phone or running water. Each night she'd walk the mile up the hill in the dark, pump her water, light a fire and her lantern and settle in for the night. She was one of the happiest people I've ever met.

The other side of the Big Sur coin was Robot. I don't think anyone knew his real name, and at times I suspected he'd forgotten it himself, long ago. From the best I could gather from his disjointed stories and explanations, he first arrived there after being discharged from the military after the Korean War. He fell in love with the place, and having no income, he settled in along the side of the road, living in his vehicle, when he had one or in a tent just

36

off the road.

He was in his late fifties when I first met him, a wild and gruff man. I was planning to surf at Fullers, a boulder-strewn, fast-peeling break at the bottom of a five hundred foot cliff. You had to really want to surf there. Well, Robot was sitting on a five gallon bucket whittling away on something when I pulled up. He offered to guard my truck for me while I was gone, for some small consideration. I thought: guard it from whom, from him probably. I declined, hiked the long and steep trail, got humbled by surf that was out of my league and finally stumbled back up the cliff to my vehicle, which was unmolested.

I looked over at the guy, seeing he was obviously threadbare and homeless, and I felt sorry for him, thinking, how hard would it have been for me to give him a few bucks. While it was too late for that, I did have a cold six pack in my cooler, so I pulled up next to him, offered him a beer and asked what he was doing.

Turned out he was carving stone, making pipes for the local dope smokers. I was fascinated and started asking questions. He showed me how it was done and ended up giving me a piece of stone and an old file, along with some verbal lessons in carving. I went home, carved a few pipes, found it to be fun, sold some to the local gift stores and then graduated to figures. A few weeks later, I carved an abstract of two people hugging, took it to the buyer at the Phoenix Shop at Nepenthe in Big Sur and she had it sold and a check in the mail to me in two weeks. And that started a short but exciting career as a sculptor.

Over the next few years, I looked Robot up whenever I was in Big Sur, which was often. For a time he had two tents set up a few yards down an embankment by the pullout just south of Fullers. He'd found a flat spot where he carved, slept and made a comfortable life. On one visit he pointed out over the ocean and down the rugged cliffs, saying he had a million dollar view that cost him nothing.

Besides carving, he would do tricks for the tourists, like balance chairs and tables on his nose. Plus he did his share of begging. I think he also had a small military pension, as I believe he'd been wounded. He was a con man, a drunk, a doper and a brawler, but he was a genuine character, a delight to hang out

37

with, a fountain of local information and a good friend. These characters, like Jaime de Angulo and Henry Miller before them, and the recent characters who came after them, make Big Sur unique.

It's really hard to define Big Sur, geographically or otherwise. As was said to a tourist once, when she asked where it was, the answer was, "Big Sur is a state of mind."

And, while that is true on one level, there is a certain geography involved, and for me Big Sur is everything between Ragged Point, just south of the Monterey County line and Carmel Highlands, at Mal Paso Creek. That's seventy plus miles.

Certainly, there are gray areas on each end, and in some local bars one could easily get into a good argument over the boundaries.

While **Ragged Point** is a great place for tourist watching—they are often dressed quite colorfully and tend to engage in enjoyable-to-observe tourist activities—it also has a distinctive feel to it. The parking lot is always busy, and it is a favorite stop for people touring by motorcycle, and the best way to see Big Sur is on a motorcycle. The place offers rooms from under $200 to almost $450. For reservations or more information Tel: (805) 927-4502 E-mail: info@raggedpointinn.net.

There is also a nice restaurant and a snack bar, art and gift gallery, minimart and wedding facilities. There is also a narrow trail in the back that leads down the sheer cliff to the beach. From past experience, I don't recommend taking that trail after a couple beers.

Across the highway and just a few yards south, an old dirt road drops down from the hills. That trail leads to a ridgeline that extends north, drops down past an abandoned mine, and ends up connecting to the trail out of Salmon Creek, a few miles north. There are a couple of camps up there, and connections to the Coast Ridge Road, which is really back country. It's not marked as a trail, but the other end, at Salmon Creek is clearly marked and well worth a day hike.

I find it's nice to just stop there for a few minutes, grab an ice cream or a burger, perhaps a beverage, sit in the sun, watch the people and take a stroll around the lovely grounds. Also, they have a restroom, a facility that isn't too common beyond there.

If you don't like twisting roads, carved out of the side of a cliff, the next few miles will not be fun. The road is hundreds of feet above the surf, and the curves are tight. The ten miles between Ragged Point and Gorda will take you twenty to thirty minutes, but beyond Gorda the road gets much better.

I'd be surprised if there are a hundred people living in and around **Gorda (M.P. 10.20)**. For the tourists, there is mainly the cafe, which serves good but slightly pricey food, the gas station and the little store. However the roads on either side of these businesses lead up to the town proper, and there's one fellow up there who sells some nice jade sculpture pieces. The road loops up and back down, so you don't have to try to turn around on a one lane road. There is also a phone booth in front of the store. No, not every cell phone will connect there or anywhere in Big Sur. You turn them on and cross your fingers.

Note to anyone who doesn't mind getting out of the car: all along the way there are signs for trail heads. Keep an eye out. You don't have to hike miles into the back country. Often a short walk will take you to some unforgettable vistas and grottoes. If you really want to explore, the Ventana Chapter of the Sierra Club puts out a great trail guide. I've been in some pretty remote places, and that guide has kept me from getting lost.

The next public place along the road, just a short drive north, is **Treebones Resort.** It's perched on a hill, overlooking the

ocean, and the rooms are yurts, each separate, connected by wooden walkways to the main lodge, restaurant and pool. If you're going to stay in southern Big Sur, this would be one of two places. Take the first right after the little town of Gorda onto Willow Creek Road (M.P. 11.10). Watch for their 'solar' Treebones sign on the right side of Hwy One. Take an immediate right through the gate and follow the half mile road to the Resort. Even if you opt not to stay, drive up and check it out. It might just seduce you. And don't let the term "yurt" put you off. These are comfortable, roomy little round cabins, most with wonderful coastal views. They have an elegant dining room with a menu sure to please any traveler.

Just past Treebones, on the left, is Willow Creek beach/cove/viewpoint (M.P. 11.66). You can park on the top, look out over the rocky beach, perhaps see some surfers getting excellent waves and also feed some bread or nuts to the ground squirrels who are so used to people, they'll crawl up on your lap to get a treat.

Another option is to drive down the short road to the beach, where you'll find another of those elusive restrooms. Willow Creek ends at the beach, or what passes for a beach. At low tide you can walk down a bit, or you can hike up the creek. On the rare calm summer day, you can actually launch a kayak there and explore one of the most rugged stretches of our coast. I managed that once, but it was spooky knowing I was alone and there was only one place for many miles to land.

A bit over a mile further, there is, at least for Big Sur, a complex. First you'll see Plaskett Creek Campground (M.P.13.56), a great place to camp if it isn't full, which isn't often. The campground offers access to Plaskett Creek Road, which you can also drive, and which goes up and up and, well, you know. You can also cross the highway and wander the bluffs, which in spring are covered with wildflowers. The campsites, on thick green grass and nestled under trees, are large and perfect for pitching a tent.

Across the road and just south of the entrance to the campground is **Sand Dollar Beach (M.P. 13.85)**, arguably the loveliest beach on the planet. Every time I look down from the bluffs, it takes my breath away, this mile-wide cove with a rocky beach and massive sea stacks jutting out at the south end. From the parking lot, which now costs five or six bucks (you can also park along the highway), a path leads down to a lookout over the beach, and just before the lookout, the trail continues down to the beach. It's a bit of a hike, including a section of stairs. You can wander and tide pool at low tide. At high tide there isn't much beach. It's also a premier surf spot. Sometimes long, rolling lines peel off from north of the big rock stack, curving in toward shore. Other times massive walls of water almost close out the bay and scare the hell out of all but the most daring surfers.

Next to the campground and across from Sand Dollar Beach is the high school. With only a handful of students, this small school serves the entire south coast of Big Sur. These kids have this vast, wild coast as their playground, so it's no wonder they don't miss having a shopping mall. In the fall the school is the site of the Big Sur Jade Fest, featuring all things jade, along with food and music and a sample of the local color. I find it impossible to visit the Jade Fest without finding something I must hAvenue

41

Next to the campground, on the south side, is Plaskett Ridge Road, a dirt road that serves some off-the-beaten-track homes and which connects to the Coast Ridge Road, which, in turn eventually connects with Nacimiento-Fergusson Road, but I don't recommend driving it. Once when camping at Plaskett with a group, two of us walked up the road and as we passed a nice house, in a clearing, surrounded by a deck, the elderly couple sitting on the deck waved to us and called us over. This was their retirement home, and although completely off the grid, they had everything: satellite phone and TV, well, generator and propane. They also had a wide defensible space, a wide swath of grass before the line of trees, something important to people living in the back country. They were both hospitable and informative people, and folks who had the life they'd planned for.

A bit further up the highway is the Pacific Valley Station (M.P. 14.70), in case you need a ranger. There is also the Prewitt Loop Trail that starts behind the station, wanders way up the mountainside and eventually loops back to the highway, some 12 miles later.

There was another restaurant and store at Pacific Valley, just up the road. Now a road goes up to a flat spot with a trailer on it and goes down the other side back to the highway. Pacific Valley burned down some years back, either by accident or foul play. However, you can pull over opposite the site and hike down the in-clined coastal bluff to a nice little cove beach, where, incidentally the surf is occasionally quite good.

Mill Creek beach access (M.P. 18.46) is the short road down from the highway just south of the Kirk Creek Campground, a campground on the bluffs. There is a very small parking and beach area there, and, trust me, you can launch a kayak there, one of the few easy to reach launching places along Big Sur. This isn't a camping area, just a parking and picnic place with benches and a restroom.

For Camping, Kirk Creek is just ahead, and since it's National Forest land, the camping is cheaper than at the state parks, but it is almost always full, so good luck. The one time I saw it virtually deserted was during the great El Nino slides of '98, when the road was washed away in two or three places, and it was almost impossible to get into Big Sur for several weeks. I came over Nacimiento-Furgusson Road through King City, Camp Hunter Liggett and over the narrow road and down to the coast. It took all day to get into Big Sur, but with all the rains, the wildflowers in Hunter Liggett, usually spectacular, where almost unworldly, and the coast was overgrown with lush, verdant, flowering foliage of all kinds. Nacimiento-Furgusson Road comes out across the high-way from Kirk Creek Camp, so when I finally made it down the hill, there were two cars in the camp, one belonging to the camp-ground host.

Since we now find ourselves parked along the road and standing at that junction, I suggest getting back in the car and driv-ing up Nacimiento-Furgusson. It's a bit over seven miles to the top, but the views along the way are impressive, rolling ridgelines, giv-ing way to deep canyons, backed by more ridgelines, and a huge swath of coast spread out below.

If you feel really ambitious, leave the car, pull off the bike and ride up. If you can make it to the top without stopping several times, you are an aerobic superstar. But either way, when you get to the top, the paved road continues down the hill toward Hunter Liggett, but on the way there are two campgrounds, Nacimiento and Ponderosa, rarely full, and a good alternative when Kirk Creek is packed.

But, if you're not ready to camp, but would rather take a wonderful hike, at the top of Nacimiento-Furgusson turn left on the dirt road to the Cone Peak trail head. Now this is five miles of really bad dirt road, so a high clearance pick up truck or a four wheeler would be best, particularly if it has rained at all recently, which makes the road almost impassible for anything. But, if you brave the road, the two and a half mile hike up to Cone Peak is worth it. There is a cement platform up there, kind of a lookout, and from there you've got 360 degrees and umpteen miles of view. On a clear day you can see Morro Rock on one end, and the greater Big Sur coast. You can also see down and over Hunter Liggett.

Limekiln State Beach (M.P. 20.76) is the next stop. It's a state park with camping, and it also has a beach, which is usually calm enough for bathing or for launching a kayak. Again, there are few places to do that, so kayakers take note.

Even though camping along the road is illegal, people camp in their cars, RVs, vans, campers all the time, along the dirt pull-outs, but not in the paved vista points. I never pay when I can stay for free, but not everyone feels that way, so I'm going to direct you to drive three or four miles further north to **Lucia (M.P. 23.00)**, perched on a cliff over the ocean. Lucia has quaint, scenic little cabins clinging to the cliffs, hundreds of feet  above a rocky cove. It's like some old world postcard, driving up and seeing those cabins seemingly hanging on the rock wall. Someone who is an avowed camper happened to stay there one night and found it the best place he'd ever stayed. They have a nice rustic restaurant with a good menu and a store. It is located next to some of the most unstable sections of the coast, and there is often road construction going on in the area. In 1998, the road just north was totally washed away, and the big earth movers were trying to create a new road bed out of a slumped mountain, and we had to sit and wait for the ten minute windows every four hours when cars could go through on a narrow piece of packed dirt hanging precariously from the cliff.

Just before reaching Lucia, there's a turnoff to New Camaldoli Hermitage, two miles up a narrow road and well worth a side trip. Run by monks, they have a book store and accommodations for retreats, a quiet place to get away, meditate and relax (http://www.contemplation.com).

There isn't much in the way of tourist stops for a few miles, but then you pass Esalen Institute (M.P. 32.40), a world famous human potential, new age, meditate and get your head on straight kind of place, but you don't just drop in. You have to reserve by signing up for one of their weekend or week long courses. You can, however, stop by check it out and ask about their programs. The location is wonderful, perched on a scenic bluff, the programs excellent and

44

the natural hot pools, legendary. I know a number of people wh swear by this place, claiming the experience can't be beat. It's a bit too pricey for my budget, so I can't speak from experience.

At last you are getting close to the heart of Big Sur. Julia Pfeiffer Burns State Park (M.P. 35.80) should be visited at least once. Park in the lot or on the highway. There is a trail from the lot, under the highway and out to a view of the much-photographed **McWay Falls** that drops 80 feet straight down to the beach. Every-

one who has passed this way has walked out there and taken a photo. I believe that having taken this photo is one's passport to Nirvana or Heaven or whatever after life reward you expect.

But the real park, the place where you can spend some time, is the other direction. Hike the Ewoldsen Trail. It follows a stream up through the redwoods, into a mixed forest and up to where you get some great views. This is a good sample of the hikes in Big Sur, and it's not particularly difficult. You can see most of it in an hour or two.

Julia Pfeiffer Burns Park also has two environmental camps on the ocean side of the highway. You can reserve these scenic walk in sites at: http://www.reserveamerica.com/campsiteFilterAction.do?sitefilter=ALL&startIdx=0&contractCode=CA.

If you are spending time hiking in Big Sur, I recommend Robert Stone's Day Hikes Around Big Sur. He has also written other books that cover parts of the central and north coast: Day Hikes Around Monterey and Carmel, Day Hikes Around San Luis Obispo and Day Hikes Around Santa Barbara. For the hiker, Robert's books make a great companion to this one.

Partington Cove (M.P. 37.85) is at a place where the highway curves inland. There are ample places to pull off on either side of the highway. Once out of the car, you'll find a road leading down toward the beach. That's Partington Cove, a place where liquor boats tied up during prohibition. The road leads down to both a small beach and a cove. The cove would be suitable for scuba diving. Exploring the area can be done in a few minutes, as there's less than a mile involved getting to both destinations.

The Tan Bark trail is on the other side of the highway, on the north side of the curve. The trail suffered some damage during the last fire, and it took around three years for the state to repair it, but now it's open again, so take some time to hike it. This is a Big Sur trail in the same way as the Roman Coliseum is a place to visit in Rome. It's one of the Big Sur hikes that always opens my mind, centers me, and leaves me immune to stress for days.

Within 50 yards of the parking spot the trail enters a wonderland, suddenly shifting from open coastal to a dense redwood forest and then to a bridge over frothy, tumbling Partington Creek. The canyon, only a couple dozen yards wide in spots, is thickly wooded and the ambient light is muted green and burnt sienna, and everything is soft and damp and cool. The creek cascades over rocks and fallen logs in a series of rapids and waterfalls. Every inch of the creek is dynamic and fascinating, making it hard to watch the trail as it climbs along the side of this musical flow of white water.

In some places the walls on both sides are bare rock, stretching up in a steep "V," dripping with hanging moss. The permanent dampness pervades all of the senses.

That first half mile or so is as beautiful as any place I've ever been. Once you've walked it, whenever someone mentions "redwood canyon," the Tan Bark image will fill your mind like a huge holographic photo. One could spend an entire day along that short stretch.

There are numerous places to step off the trail and down to a rock at creek side, to sit and watch the little waterfalls or perhaps take a photo.

A bit more than a half mile in, the trail abruptly turns away from the creek and starts to climb up the canyon wall. The trail is wet from the tiny feeder creeks that trickle down the canyon. In a short, steep section, you leave the canyon floor and then the trail levels out again. Up on the high southern edge of the canyon the forest becomes mixed and sunny. It heads back toward the highway again, and before it turns inland again, you can climb a few feet up a side trail and look down at your starting place. After heading inland, the trail turns again into a redwood forest, as it climbs high above the south fork of the creek. The trail runs along the steep side of the canyon, and each time you pause, the water music whispers from below.

Near the top of the canyon the trail crosses the creek near the headwaters, where it is a narrow and gentle trickle. There, along the creek, at the junction of two branches of the south fork, in a grove of majestic old redwoods, there was a bench made of split redwood logs. On one early spring visit, the bench was gone, and I'd considered trying to rebuild it myself. On my next visit a makeshift replacement bench had been set in place. A recent fire has left it charred. Common courtesy among the frequent hikers is, for the sake of solitude, that if you'd enjoyed the bench for a time, you'd move on when the next person comes along, allowing him or her time to meditate on the natural world.

This is a solitary, reflective place, one so soothing and serene, so bucolic and peaceful that it can do for the psyche what weekly massages and therapy can never do. It's a spot that can give the harried soul a loving caress. You need only spend a quarter hour there to be renewed. If you are artistic, you return from the bench ready to paint a picture, compose a song, write a poem, or pen a novel. If you are a lover, you return ready to buy a ring and commit.

Those in a hurry can return along the same path, but continuing a while longer rewards the hiker with another magical spot.

The trail continues upward for perhaps another 20 minutes, out of the shaded redwood groves, into the mixed forest, with occasional ocean vistas. Then, shortly after the trail turns downhill, it merges with a fire road. A right turn leads steeply down the wooded road to Highway One at M.P. 37.00, and an almost mile walk along the highway back to the car.

Almost everyone, however, goes left for a quarter mile

detour to the old Tin House. The Tin House was built by a friend of F.D.R. during World War II, as a place where the President could get away from it all. F.D.R. never stayed there, and the place, closed up, now belongs to the state.

To reach it, walk down the fire road to the left for a few yards, and then turn sharply to the right for a short, steep descent to the Tin House

While the house itself is interesting, the real reward to the hiker hides behind the house. There is a beautiful meadow that slopes down and then drops sharply away to the sea. This is the place to pull off the day pack, unpack the lunch, and enjoy a sweeping view of the best of the Big Sur coast.

If you are taking this hike in the spring, that meadow is green, fragrant and filled with flowers. Also, the shaded part of the lower section of the fire road, just above the highway, will be ablaze in wildflowers. If you go in the heat of late spring or early summer, bring insect repellent; the flies and gnats can be fierce. The upside is that the warm weather brings out thousands of butterflies that can become so thick that the air in front of you appears to dance like heat waves in the desert.

The hike, excluding the walk back down the highway, is about 6 miles, a good half day excursion.

Even the trip back to the parking area can be memorable. Across the road from the bottom of the fire road is a scenic pullout where you can look toward the famous McWay Falls at Julia Pfeiffer Beach.

Walk back on the ocean side, facing cars, both for safety and for glimpses of crashing waves. Or, if you come with friends, bring two cars and leave one at the scenic pullout, thus avoiding an unappealing mile walk on the road.

The hiker on a tight schedule can make the loop in three hours. For a leisurely walk with lunch, allow four or five.

Everyone loves to poke around an art gallery, and **Coast Gallery (M.P. 40.90)**, a short drive further north, is one I never tire of stopping at. For a long time the little cafe upstairs was closed, but now it's open, serving coffee, beer, soft drinks, snacks and sandwiches. The cafe is a reason to stop; the gallery is a reason to linger.

In the round upstairs chamber they have a collection of Henry Miller's art. Yes, the famous writer, banned for years in his home country, was also a prolific and talented watercolorist. Naturally, after he died, his work skyrocketed in value. They also have other artists and the main downstairs room has wonderful bronze pieces.

There is also great glass and wooden pieces. They even sell music, and it was the place I first heard Loreena McKennitt, now one of my favorites.

If you didn't stop for the night back in Lucia, you have another chance. Deetjen's Big Sur Inn is just ahead (M.P. 43.17). The place has a wonderful, story book history, and I'm sure the people there would be glad to fill you in. It's a European, Scandinavian-looking, little inn in the redwoods. The old world restaurant has delicious food, and a décor that makes you think of a mountain chalet in the Alps, They have rustic cabins, under the shade of ancient redwoods, each one complete with a cat. This place fairly oozes charm. They also have a wonderful breakfast and lovely waitresses.

**Henry Miller Memorial Library** (M.P. 43.50) is no more than a short walk from Deetjen's. This, in recent years, has become the heart of the Big Sur coast.

Since Magnus Thoren, a transplant from Sweden, took over as director, the library's mandate has expanded. There are musical and cultural events on a regular basis, open mic nights, and in the summer, the International Short Film Festival, the best film festival I've ever attended. To give you an idea how much of a "must stop" this place is, on a typical day in summer, you're apt to encounter a number of European tourists who have planned their travel in California around a stop here. Miller is highly regarded in much of Europe, and he was my first literary influence, which just adds to my connection to the library. Tell the wonderful people working there that I told you to stop by and buy a book. Besides Miller, many excellent authors are represented there. You might even pick up one of mine.

Even if there is no performance, film, musical interlude or anything like that, the grounds are lovely, and the building, once the home of Miller's friend Emil White, is filled with wonderful books, books you might not see in your typical bookstore. Grab some coffee, buy a book, and sit in the yard, surrounded with delightful sculptures and read for a time. There is no hurry to continue on. They even have a computer with internet access that you can use for free or drop some change in the donation box. Do check out the sculpture, Y2K in the yard, a wire cable figure on a cross of old computer monitors.

The Hawthorne Gallery is just ahead (M.P. 43.90). A fairly new place, it has some really large pieces, such as $50,000 glass and steel tables. "Who," you say, "would spend 50 grand on a table?" One look and you'd know that if you had the money, you'd buy it without thinking twice.

Just up the hill and on the ocean side of the road is the Nepenthe restaurant, Phoenix shop and **Cafe Kevah** (M.P. 43.90). Where to begin? Well walk up the winding ramps and steps to

Nepenthe, order an $15 burger, or an expensive full meal, or you can do what I usually do, order a beer, sit out on the patio and take in the view of miles of the south Big Sur coast and suck up the ambiance. Nepenthe is almost at the top of the hill, and then the restaurant is a walk further up, so the view from the glass walled restaurant or the patio, where drinks and appetizers are served, as well as occasional entertainment (belly dancers on my last visit), is over a cascading landscape, ending at the water.

If you don't have time for that, Cafe Kevah is just above the Phoenix Shop, and you can get a muffin and coffee with your view. But since you have to skirt the entrance to the shop to get there, stop in and look around. The Phoenix Shop is a small wonder. It has a book section, jewelry, arts and crafts, clothing and too many other things to list.

I have a special place in my heart for the Phoenix Shop. Years ago, after Robot taught me the basics of carving stone, I sold my first piece of sculpture there.     However, the practical reason for a tourist to stop there is that if you need a gift for someone back home, you can't help finding just the right thing here.

At the top of the hill you'll see an old house, marking the entrance to the Ventana Inn and Spa. Across the road is a newer place, Post Ranch (M.P. 44.90). Now, the Ventana Inn's rooms, stretched along the hillside, each with a balcony and a view even better than Nepenthe, aren't cheap. One night there cost four times as much as my first car, when I was in high school, and there are rooms at the Post Inn that are several times more costly. If you can afford the glass/steel table at the Hawthorne, these places' prices won't scare you. It is, none the less, one of the great experiences for the traveler. The restaurant there is first class.

For the camper, Ventana had a beautiful campground down by the creek, nestled in a grove of redwoods. The campground is closed now, and I don't know when it will reopen, but there are several others in the next six miles.

The parking lot below the restaurant and inn is the jumping off point for the **Coast Ridge Road**. Locals and rangers have keys to the gates. The rest of us hike, but put in four miles, and you'll have some of the best views anywhere, including majestic Mount Manuel and Point Sur. There are a few homes at the top, and just

beyond that is a great place to stop for lunch and a 360 degree view. A few more steps; you're in the **Ventana Wilderness.**

The Big Sur Garden Gallery, also the Spirit Garden (M.P. 45.20), is on the left as you start down the hill. The garden is interesting, as is just about any stop in Big Sur. The plus is that you'll always meet the kind of interesting people you'll not find at home. There is also the bakery there, with pizza, sandwiches, beer and wine, and they have eclectic entertainment there every week, people with exotic names, people you probably never heard of but will enjoy if you're there when they have a show.

As you're dropping down the hill, look for a turn off heading down to the **Pfeiffer Beach (M.P. 46.20)**. It used to be free, but now there's a manned booth and a five dollar fee, but the beach is really worth wandering. There's a cove on the south side that actually has good surf from time to time. There's a longer beach on the north, and in between are rock stacks with two arches, more square holes in them where the tide and waves roll through

and in the late afternoon, the sun glows through. They get photographed a lot, so if you go into many places in the area, you're bound to see a picture of it. Getting there involves a very narrow, two mile road, trailers and RVs not allowed, but it's one of the few

accessible beaches, and it has a wild, mystical charm about
love to walk along it early in the morning, just as the mist is lifting,
and a few people in sleeping bags on the beach are slowly waking.
A small canyon leading back from the beach has a stately cypress,
and as the morning mist is dissolving, it's bathed in streamers of
light.

The Big Sur Deli and the Bazaar are by the post office
(M.P. 45.30). You can get a snack and coffee and mail out those
postcards, before stopping at the Multi-Agency Ranger Station
(M.P. 46.40), on the inland side of the road. Clean restrooms, good
tips on local hikes and a selection of local guidebooks, make for a
good reason to stop. You can also park and hike the Pine Ridge
Trail, which runs along the Big Sur River, and if you are up for it,
Sykes Hot Springs is a quick ten miles up the trail, and the hot
springs will take away the ache of the hike. Or, you could go half
way, turn right on the Terrace Creek Trail and connect with the
Coast Ridge Road and return to the parking area at the Ventana
Inn, a ten mile loop, requiring a car at both ends.

Pfeiffer Big Sur State Park (M.P. 47.20) is the state park
camping area. It is a beautiful park, with over two hundred campsites strewn out along the Big Sur River, some under the redwoods
and some in clearings. Since it's part of the California State Park
system, they take reservations, so reserve early or come in the off-
season. Besides camping, they have **lodge cabins** that are wonderful and rustic,
with no damn
TV to drown
out the sounds
of the forest.
The restaurant
is also excel-
lent, with a
breakfast that
will hold you
for the whole
day. They also

have a camp store, complete with a selection of fine wines, a gift
shop and Pfeiffer Falls, accessible from a parking lot just up from

the lodge. The direct walk up the creek is closed, but hike up toward Valley View, and at a junction, you can hike down to the falls. Then back at the junction, go the rest of the way to Valley View for a view of the valley.

There are other hikes in the park, including the 4 plus mile, 4,000-foot climb/hike up to **Mount Manuel,** the towering peak

that rises over the park. And, in summer, hike a quarter mile past the last camp site, over some boulders to a great swimming hole.

Bordering Pfeiffer State Park, and just a short drive south is Fernwood Campground, at the Fernwood Resort (M.P. 47.30)— (831) 667-2422 — a 60-unit campground and an 12 unit motel with fireplaces located in a redwood forest along the Big Sur River. Also along this stretch of road is The Big Sur Campground & Cabins (M.P. 49.00)—(831) 667-2322, offering tent camping with hot showers, RV camping with water and electric hook-ups as well as a dump station. Riverside Campground & Cabins (M.P. 48.90)— (831) 667-2414, is a 16-acre dog friendly property that offers RV and tent camping as well as 11 cozy cabins.

Glen Oaks with 15 fireside rooms, 7 cabin/cottages and Ripplewood, with cabins right on the river are both at (M.P. 48.30).

I love the **Fernwood Resort, bar and Redwood Grill,** just

**Author**

north of the state park. This is a place where the locals come to have a drink and share tall tales and perhaps grab a burger. The

54

food is the most reasonable along the Big Sur coast. Sometimes on the weekends, they have a local band playing, and these are always a delight. After a long hike, I have to stop here and get a pint of Dragon Slayer IPA before heading home. In the same building, a fairly new store called the Coast Ridge Outfitter sells all the stuff you'll need to trek around in the woods and mountains. If you camp at Fernwood, in one of their large sites, it's only 70 steps up to the bar and restaurant.

I keep thinking of the Big Sur Roadhouse as new, but it's been there for a few years now. I haven't dined there, but I notice they advertise happy hour from I believe 3:00 to 5:00 daily.

Along this stretch of highway, there's a concentration of places, as this is the heart of the Big Sur valley. You turn inland just after Nepenthe, go over the hill and drop into the valley, and you don't come out again until the Big Sur makes its final turn to the beach, at Andrew Molera State Park.

Ripplewood, Big Sur Roadhouse, Glen Oaks, Riverside Campground, Big Sur Campground and cabins, and the River Inn complex are all in the valley. I usually stop at the River Inn (M.P. 49.30), but I spent a weekend once at the Riverside Campground with a buddy, and we met a woman who was campground host for a time, and we had a delightful evening with beer, a warm fire and the running river at our feet.

The **River Inn** has it all: restaurant, cabins, lodge, pool, store, bar, shops, art gallery, gas station and a gift shop that has some really interesting, eclectic items. The  lady who owns it has been there for years.

I believe having lunch on the deck in the summer, when they have music, is a perfect way to spend an afternoon. Or, sometimes I'll just order a pint and walk down from the deck across the grass to the river, only a few inches deep in summer, and sit in one of the wicker chairs placed in the water, with my feet in the current, dappled light through the trees overhead, the sound of running water, the chirping of birds and the laughter of children creating the ideal music to sip a beer to.

Stop by the Local Color Gallery, off the parking lot. You might find a cheap treasure that will someday be valuable. I picked up an original Helen Jerene watercolor there once for sixty-five bucks. She is fabulous, and her works runs into the many hundreds and even thousands now.

You have another couple miles of redwoods before arriving at Andrew Molera State Park (M.P. 51.20). First you'll cross the Juan Higuera Bridge, which is where low paid workers who can't afford the expensive rents spend the night. Don't stop. Just take my word for it.

Andrew Molera State Park has always been a special place to me. My first memory of the place was from the early 70s. The park was a recent addition to the state system and still unimproved. The parking lot and most of the trails were not in place. The old dirt road through the meadow to the beach was a remnant from when the park was a working ranch.

We walked the mile to the beach and the **mouth of the Big Sur River**. Even then, the surfers had discovered it, and three guys with boards were camped out on the headland at the point. Otherwise, the area was deserted. The park was a chaos of meadow and forest. I imagined it to be as it was when the Esselen Indians had it to themselves.

In 1834 Juan Bautista Alvarado, the future governor of California, got a land grant of almost 9,000 acres from the Mexican government. The land stretched from the Little Sur River to Cooper Point. In 1840 Alvarado traded Rancho El Sur to Captain John Rogers Cooper. The land was passed down to his children, eventually to a daughter who married E.J. Molera, whose son was Andrew Molera.

It was a working farm, dairy and cattle ranch for many

years. Upon Andrew's death, his sister Frances took control of the property, selling it to the Nature Conservancy in 1965, while retaining occupancy and grazing privileges until her death in 1968. The land was transferred to the State, but remained a working ranch until 1972, about the time I first visited.

The park has **24 walk in camp sites** about a third of a mile from the parking lot. Having to walk to camp discourages people with heavy camping gear, so one can find a site at Molera when other areas are full.

The numbered sites are a fairly recent change. Originally, there was just the large meadow, and campers would find a spot a comfortable distance from the next camper and set up a tent. In the 80s, it cost a dollar to camp, and often the camper would have cleared out before the ranger came around to collect. There were a couple of outhouses and no potable water.

Now one gets an actual site, and it costs $10 per night, last time I checked, still a bargain compared to the rest of Big Sur. Remember, California is hurting for money, and camping fees keep going up, so don't hold me to the $10 price.

For day use, one can pay the $6 parking fee or park on the highway and walk in.

There are nearly 30 miles of trails in the park. Many people simply walk from the parking lot to the beach, a two mile round trip. For the adventurous hiker who wants spectacular views, the Ridge Bluff 8 mile loop is outstanding. The preferred route is to cross the river and take the River Trail to the Hidden Trail, a steep three quarters of a mile climb to the Ridge Trail. Then it's a gradual climb on a dirt road to the top, at over 1,000 foot elevation. There's a bench at the top, affording a **view of the park,** Point Sur, Pico

Blanco and Post Summit. It's a great place for photography and lunch.

Return via the Bluff Trail, which wanders down toward the beach, through wild flowers and coastal brush. It affords a continually stunning view, and there are side trails to secluded pockets of beach. The trail back to the parking lot intersects the bottom of the Bluff Trail, but a few yards further is the beach, a must stop on a sunny day.

There is also a trail on the east side of the highway, a few dozen yards south of the entrance. This climbs almost 1600 feet in 2.5 miles before exiting the park and continuing on another 2 miles and 1600 more feet to the top of Post Summit. This is a very strenuous hike, best saved for a cool day. Each time I've hiked it, I've promised myself it was the last time, but one day I'll forget the pain and probably do it again.

For people who want to explore without hiking, Molera Horseback Tours will guide you along the river, meadows and along the beach. You can reserve a horse in advance or simply show up.

There is also fishing in the river and ocean and a sheltered surf spot at the mouth of the river, where the waves wrap around Cooper Point. Also, there is parking on the highway, in a direct line to Cooper's cabin, making the trip to the beach a bit shorter and saving you six bucks.

Directly across the road from the entrance to Molera is the Old Coast Road. Once upon a time you couldn't get over Bixby Canyon, not until the government built Highway One during the depression, because the road was needed and people needed the work. So, the old, dirt road turned inland at Bixby Canyon and wandered twelve miles through woods, over creeks and over high ridges before coming down to the coast again at Andrew Molera. It's passable, except perhaps during heavy rains. People live up there and drive it daily. Also, somewhere near the mid point is the trailhead for the Little Sur Trail, which goes to Pico Blanco Public Camp and beyond. You can even hike up to the top of Pico Blanco, named for the pale granite top, but that's on private land, so I'm not telling you to do it and get one of the best views in Big Sur.

Also, for you surfers, drive perhaps a half mile up the Old Coast Road from Molera until you find a wide spot and pull over on the ocean side. You'll have a view of the cove and surf, saving a long surf check hike. It's also a great place to unpack the lunch and look over the point and Andrew Molera Park.

Once north of Molera Park, there are twenty miles of lovely, almost open coast before reaching Carmel. Pfeiffer Point is that big rock with a lighthouse on the top (M.P. 54.10). It's now a State Historic Park. There are tours available: November through March Saturdays and Sundays: 10 AM, Wednesdays: 1 PM. April through October Satur-days and

**Mouth of Little Sur**

59

Wednesdays: 10 AM and 2 PM Sundays: 10 AM. The tours are ten bucks for adults. They also have moonlight tours on full moon nights, and these are $15.

Soon you wind down to the bridge over the Little Sur River (M.P. 56.00), and then you wind way up again to Hurricane Point (M.P. 58.00), named for the wind that howls most of the time. The turn out, high above the rocky shore, is a favorite place to take a photo. Then you drop down to the Bixby Bridge (M.P 59.50), one of the most photographed bridges in the country. On the south side of the bridge is the other end of the Old Coast Road, heading back toward Molera Park.

At about milepost 61.70, a road leads off inland. That's Palo Colorado, and it goes up a stream canyon, past some lovely cabins and after about five miles to Mill Creek County Park. You'll need a permit to hike there, so see Monterey Peninsula Regional Parks District. Or you can continue to the end of the road, something over seven miles to Bottcher's Gap. There's a small parking fee, and then you can take the trail (north side of parking lot) up to Skinner Ridge, where you get a great view of both the ocean and "the window," that notch in the mountain that gives the range its name, Ventana. It's about 2.5 miles up to the top, and then the trail drops down to a junction. At that point you can climb again toward Devil's Peak and Mount Carmel, a really steep climb, or head down to Apple and Turner Creek camps. If you keep hiking down, you'll eventually get out of the woods and on Long Valley Road, which will take you back to Palo Colorado Rd. at the half way point, called the Hoist (note the hoist on the long beam). If you want to do the whole thing, leave one car at the Hoist and drive another to the top.

Just north of Palo Colorado, at the top of the hill, is Rocky Point Restaurant (M.P. 61.90). OK, it's pretty expensive, but the views are great, and at night they have flood lights aimed at the rocks below, and when the waves break into them, it's freakin' beautiful. When I get in the mood, I just go into the bar, buy a beer, enjoy the view and eat somewhere less expensive.

There is a wide spot along the ocean side of the highway, room for dozens of cars, and trails running down to the beach. That's **Garrapata State Beach** (M.P. 63.00). In the spring, the wildflowers along the coastal bluffs are wonderful, but be careful

of the poison oak.

Also, at about milepost 66.80 there's a line of trees on the in-land side, along with an old building. That's Soberanes Canyon, one of the most popular hiking spots on the Big Sur Coast. You've got a couple of choices here. You can head up the canyon, through an unexpected grove of cactus and into the redwood forest. In about three miles the trail leaves the forest and goes straight up possibly the steepest half mile you'll ever hike. That takes you to the top of **Rocky Ridge**, which can also be reached from the Rocky Ridge trail, a few dozen yards north of the canyon, off the

highway. The Rocky Ridge Trail is perhaps the fifth steepest trail you'll ever hike, but it's ok to stop and catch your breath, because every step of the trail offers vistas that will blow your mind. If you do this in early spring, I can promise the richest assortment of vivid wildflowers you'll find anywhere.

The two trails meet at the top, but about three fourths of the way up the Rocky Ridge Trail, and just a few feet off the trail, is a bench, set up on a pile of rocks. From there you look straight down on Big Sur and even Carmel Highlands and Point Lobos.

About three miles north, you cross the bridge at Mal Paso Creek and enter Carmel Highlands, three miles of gorgeous coast covered with gorgeous homes. Also, along the way, you'll see Highlands Inn. It's a pretty high-end place to stay, but the ambiance is special.

**Point Lobos State Reserve** (M.P. 70.20) is where the greater Big Sur coast really ends and Carmel and the Monterey Peninsula starts.

You can park on the highway and walk in, or you can pay the ten bucks and drive in.

Everyone should walk along the shore and bluffs of Point Lobos at least once in their lives. I've done it dozens, maybe even a hundred times, and it always sends my spirit soaring. Whalers Cove, the first turn off you come to when you enter, has a launch ramp, where kayaks and scuba divers enter the water. If you kayak, do this one in summer and make sure the swell is quite small. You can paddle out and around the point, putting you up close to Stellar Sea Lions, grizzly bears with fins, but when a swell of any size is up, the point becomes a giant washing machine and it can be scary and even dangerous. I went out with a fairly experienced kayaker once, and as we rounded the point, he absolutely refused to go one stroke further.

But, hike up the steps from Whalers, and follow the trail along the edge of the cliffs, noting the cormorants nesting just a few feet away on the sea stacks and the deer wandering through the

62

brush. Follow it until it reaches the next parking lot, and then hike out to the end of the point and the beach, and then keep going along a section of shore with beautifully folded rocks, uplifted at the time the coastal mountains were formed. Then keep going to China Beach and Bird Rock, which has a side path to close up views of nesting sea birds and finally to the gentle, almost hidden Gibson Beach. From there, you can take a trail through the woods, straight back to the entrance.

When you head north from Point Lobos, you'll cross the Carmel River (M.P. 72.33) and enter the greater Monterey Peninsula.

# Monterey Bay

The Monterey Bay has been my home for several years. It really has a bit of everything: mountains, forests, rivers and water-falls, beaches with great surf, bays, estuaries, scenery and nightlife. I can paddle among wildlife, take a hike and be home in time to change and go out to hear a great band or catch an art film.

When I first arrived, I did what I always do in new digs, I explored, and by "explored" I mean wandering all the back roads and mountain lanes, hiking all the local trails, visiting all the ob-scure places, rather like a dog sniffing every rock, tree and gopher hole.

I managed to find all the micro brewpubs, some of the bet-ter ones now gone forever. Also, since I love redwoods, exploring the dark and surrealistically primal Santa Cruz Mountains was a priority. Then there was Elkhorn Slough, a biologically rich brack-ish system that extends over five miles from the ocean to where it loses itself in mud flats. It sits at the midpoint of the Bay. There were also the Monterey and Pacific Grove coasts, picture post card coastlines, perfect for kayaking. Then, of course, there's Santa Cruz, where the politics play like an old Monty Python skit.

I remember taking a drive shortly after settling in. I was on one of the back roads in the Bonny Doon area. I think it was either Empire Grade or Smith Grade, way out in the woods, hardly a sign of human habitation. Cruising slowly under towering redwoods, I suddenly heard a strange sound, a semi-melodious squawking, sounding oddly like bagpipes. I slowed even more, and then be-tween the trees marched a man dressed in full Scottish garb, kilt and all, bagpipes in his arm and blowing up a storm. I stopped, and when he came abreast of me, I waved him over. After a question of two I learned that he was playing pibroch, a rarely heard 17th cen-tury Highland marching music. And why was he doing this out in the middle of the woods? He pointed at his bagpipes and nodded. Indeed, I thought, where else could he get away with playing?

Even before moving here, I used to come over from my in-land home on weekends, and in the process developed my almost perfect day. I'd drive to Monterey, unload my kayak, and paddle along Cannery Row and Pacific Grove. Then I'd unload my bike and ride along the extensive bike and walking trail that extends all along the Monterey/Pacific Grove coast, stopping perhaps for coffee or at one of the art galleries along the way. Then, as I had managed to work up a good appetite, I would stop at one of the seafood restaurants along Cannery Row and get a window seat over the tide pools and have lunch and a cold ale. If I managed to stay late enough, I'd stop by the old Doc Ricketts Lab, a little club on the Row and catch whatever local band was playing.

The other alternative was to head to Santa Cruz, surf Pleasure Point in Capitola and go into downtown Santa Cruz for lunch and, naturally, the requisite ale.

But, please excuse me. I believe I left you coming out to Point Lobos, heading into Carmel. Well, when you cross the Carmel River you come to something you haven't seen for well over a hundred miles, a traffic light. That's Rio Road, and if you turn right you'll see a small, cute shopping center. They have a supermarket and drug store, but forget about those. The Crossroads has some nice little shops and places to eat. One of these eateries is the Sea Harvest, owned by a group of fishermen, which means the fish is fresh and delicious. If you like seafood, you'll love this place. You can also find both fine dining and a burger place, or just a good Latte. Then walk around, and you might wander into a little men's store, in which you can see a dress shirt that costs $550 and a leather bomber jacket at $3700. Don't even ask about the jeans. Get back on Rio Road, turn left on Carmel Rancho Lane and left again on Clock Tower Place. That will take you intoThe Barnyard, a quaint old-fashioned looking shopping and eating area. There used to be great art galleries there and a wonderful bookstore, but the place is kind of drying up, with some empty storefronts. However, the Carmel Art Institute is there.

I think ten miles inland still qualifies as being at the coast, so let me introduce you to Carmel Valley. Carmel Valley Road, one signal north of Rio Road goes much further than ten miles, but that's as far as we go this trip. Ten miles in is Carmel Valley Village. You can keep going to Cachagua Road and up to the dam, where you can hike up the Carmel River into the wilderness, but

66

perhaps that's too much information. If you want more info on some of these hikes, see www.ventanawild.org or the Sierra Club web site.

Carmel Valley Road, particularly in spring, is just about as scenic a road as you'll find, and it's no wonder that there are many expensive homes and wealthy people here. There's a great fruit and veggie stand about 4-5 miles in and then the Mid Valley Center, where you can get really good coffee. At 8.6 miles, you'll see **Garland Ranch Regional Park** on the right. If you are a hiker, you should stop for a few hours. If you are a hiker and it is March or April, a stop is mandatory.

This is a hiking destination that attracts a dedicated band of regulars. While there is a core of folks who hike and run there weekly, Garland is never more popular than in the spring, when a stunning mix of dozens of species of wildflowers blanket both valley floor and hillsides.

A good way to get a cross section of this 4,500-acre park, with a good selection of the many flowers the park has to offer is to hike from the river to the top, a half day hike that gives a good aerobic workout and a visual feast.

The park starts at the Carmel River. There is parking off the side of the road, and near the parking area is a bridge over the river. Once on the park side of the river, follow the sign to the left for 200 yards to the visitor center, the best jumping-off place for exploring the western end of the park.

From the visitor center, take the trail that leads across the meadow directly toward the thickly wooded hills. In the spring, this meadow is a blinding mix of yellow poppies and blue lupine. As the trail rises, turn left on the Lupine Loop, where you'll see owl's clover, Blue Dicks, vetch, Miner's lettuce, red Clintonia and

67

Western blue-eyed grass. Bay and buckeye trees tower overhead.

After about a half mile the Lupine Loop trail intersects the Mesa Trail. Now the climbing begins. In addition to the flowers seen below, you'll start to notice Indian paint brush and the occasional wild iris. When you stop to catch your breath, look down at the valley spread out below you.

At the intersection with the Sky Trail, it's worth another 10 to 15 minutes along the Mesa Trail to the mesa itself, with fields of flowers and a small pond. Or save that for the way down and continue up the Sky Trail, where the Indian paint brush along with other flowers, grows in big clumps at almost every turn.

I know I said this before, but this is really where the climb seriously begins, and on a hot day it can be strenuous, so make sure you have plenty of water. However, the advantage of this steep trail is that you'll want to stop often to admire the vistas, which expand at every stop.

The top of the Sky Trail is over 1,800 feet, and looking down, you feel you're almost directly above the valley floor. From the small bench at the top, you can see miles of the valley, plus parts of the Salinas Valley over the top of the next range of hills. The top is a hillside meadow, complete with dozens of tiny flowers, a good place to simply lie down in the shade of a tree or in the warmth of the sun and hear the buzzing of thousands of busy insects. From this vantage point, the top of Snively's Ridge, you can look south over another valley and to the Ventana Range in Big Sur.

On the way down, if you've already taken a side trip to the Mesa, pick up the Fern Trail, which goes up a bit before heading down a shaded canyon to a charming little pond with a bench, a perfect place to cool off and look for frogs, before heading down to rejoin the Mesa Trail near the bottom.

As you near the bottom of the Mesa Trail, there are three other interesting options for extending your hike. You can detour left to Siesta Point, an overlook directly above the valley. It's a good place to admire the view or take photos. You can also take the Buckeye Nature trail back to where it intersects the Lupine Loop and the trail across the meadow to the visitor center. This trail has periodic signs informing hikers about the type of native flora along

68

the trail.

Instead of going left, you can take a right on the Cliff Trail, clearly marked, and walk along a narrow trail overlooking the valley, below outcroppings of colorful rock with ferns and other small plants growing from the cracks, before arriving at the Waterfall Trail and a short hike to the waterfall, in a shaded grotto, which will be flowing until summer. If you stay on the Waterfall Trail, you head back up to the mesa, but by backtracking you end up at the junction of the Sycamore Trail and the Lupine Loop, either giving you a pleasant stroll back to the visitor center.

If you have more than one day to spend, remember that this hike involves a small part of this vast park. East of the mesa there is a lovely redwood canyon and several more miles of trails.

There is no charge to use the park, and a mile further up Carmel Valley Road is the village of Carmel Valley, with several places to dine. If you choose to stay in Carmel Valley, you'll find enough trails in the park for at least three full days. Grab a trail guide at the visitor center if you're planning several hikes.

If you plan to stay, there is lodging in Carmel Valley. Among these are: Los Laureles Lodge, (831) 659-2233; Blue Sky Lodge, (831) 659-2256 or 800 549-2256; Country Garden Inns (831) 659-5361 or 800-367-3336, and there is a Riverside Campground at Carmel Valley Road and Schulte Rd. There is also a great little bar and grill in the village, on Carmel Valley Road, the Running Iron Restaurant & Saloon. This is the place to meet the local color and enjoy a cool drink. I always get into an interesting conversation at the bar.

Go back to Highway One on Carmel Valley Road, turn right to the next light at Ocean Street and turn left, you'll head into the heart of Carmel. Once past San Carlos Street, the main part of town starts, so start looking for a parking place. If you like art, there are more galleries in a 20 block area than just about any place you can imagine. And while you're there, there are dozens of first-class restaurants of every ethnic type. However, if you want to keep it simple or just have a good lunch, the **Village Corner** at 6th and Dolores is a long time favorite of mine. They have some basic food, plus Italian and Greek dishes. Also, there's a small restaurant, Basil, on San Carlos, between Ocean and 7th, One of the few

places this side of Tuscany that has squid ink pasta. Yum!

Ocean runs down a steep hill to the ocean and a deep, white sand beach. From the main beach, if the tide isn't too high, you can walk down to Stillwater Cove in Pebble Beach, famous for the 17 Mile drive. The beach ends at Pebble Beach Country Club, a really big and very expensive mecca for golfers.

You can drive along the beach, head south and around a point to Carmel River Beach, but on the way, you'll pass **Tor House with Hawk Tower**, the home of poet Robinson Jeffers, located at 26304 Ocean View Avenue, just a block up from the beach.
Jeffers built the place by hand, and it's pretty impressive. They offer tours on Saturdays.

At **Carmel River Beach,** you'll see how a group of conservation organizations and some public agencies restored the river mouth. If you have a kayak, and the mouth isn't breached, you can paddle up the river. If not, there are some walking trails. When you're standing on the beach, looking south, that wonderful jumble of rocky

cliffs just ahead is Point Lobos. Carmel River State Beach, also accessible from just north of Point Lobos, has a great walking trail along the water, with mansions up on the hillside, and an historic cross overlooking the river mouth.

You can drive back up to Hwy. One to get to the Monterey area or spend something like ten bucks to take the 17 Mile Drive through Pebble Beach, an interesting drive, but a better bike ride.

Besides being the home of my almost perfect day, consisting of kayaking and snorkeling, followed by a bike ride and lunch beside the water, Monterey is one of my favorite cities. It is steeped in California history—just wander around the greater downtown area and see for yourself. It also has a lovely heart of town, Alvarado Street, which ends at the Plaza and the Portola Hotel and the Monterey Convention Center. There are a couple of great art galleries in the same building as the hotel, and Peter B's Brewpub, with great ales and food, is also in the complex.

The Portola is an upscale hotel, and there's another one that's really nice, the Monterey Plaza Hotel on Cannery Row, right on the water, with wonderful views.

The Monterey Plaza hosts a number of events during the warm months, art and craft fairs, and things of that type. Off the plaza is the Museum of Monterey. Adjacent to that is Fisherman's Wharf, with a great assortment of sea food restaurants.

On the plaza, you can rent bikes or those things you pedal that will hold your whole family. The paved trail runs between the museum and the wharf and goes out to Lovers Point Park to the west and all the way to Seaside on the east.

Also, about a block east of the wharf and the harbor is Monterey Bay Kayaks, where you can rent a kayak for a paddle along Cannery row or take a guided tour. It was there where a friend and I first rented kayaks on a lark. After fifteen minutes, I told her I'd be buying one, because otherwise I would be spending all my money renting. I was totally sold and an instant avid kayaker.

Out on Fisherman's Wharf, you can go out whale watching, and you almost never fail to see whales, orcas and dolphins. Knowledgeable naturalists talk about what's out there, along with some natural history. I recommend Monterey Bay Whale Watch

84 Fisherman's Wharf # 1, (831) 375-4658

Monterey is a good walking town, particularly in the visitor-serving area. You can walk from the Plaza the few blocks to the start of **Cannery Row**, wander along the shops, watering holes, including the Cannery Row Brewing Company at 95 Prescott Avenue, and restaurants,  such as Bubba Gump, to the Monterey Bay Aquarium at the far end. And, if you are visiting Monterey, the aquarium is a must see. This is a world-class facility, but try to catch it on a weekday, as it can get pretty crowded. I won't even try to tell you all the memorable things there are to see there, but you will become intimately familiar with the plants and animals that make up the Monterey Bay. I've seen them from the water with a mask and snorkel, and **the Aquarium** experience is almost the same.

 After leaving the aquarium, walk up the hill to Lighthouse Avenue and walk back toward downtown. Then, when you return to the Plaza, wander up Alvarado and back Calle Principal, and go up Pacific Avenue to see more historic buildings from California's early days when Monterey was the capitol.

If you go west on Lighthouse, it will turn into Central Avenue in Pacific Grove. Continue driving for a mile until you see the

PG Museum of Natural History. This is a great place to while away an hour, and when there, drop a couple bucks in the jar to keep it going. They have just about every bird you could find on the Central Coast, stuffed and easy to identify.

Then go up the hill to Lighthouse, yes, same name, different town and a block apart. This is where all the stores and restaurants are. It's just small town America, with coffee places, book stores and restaurants. After you've checked it out, go back down the hill until you reach the bay and turn left. You can follow the road around past Point Pinos, with great tide pools at low tide, and the lighthouse, clear around to Asilomar State Beach and Asilomar Conference Grounds. If you ever get the chance to attend a conference here, do it. There is something about this place that makes me feel good. It seems to epitomize the combination of beauty and culture that is our central coast. The rustic buildings are set among the dunes, in thickets of cypress trees, with walking paths. Individuals may stay there when there isn't a conference, but you'll have to check http://www.visitasilomar.com/accommodations.aspx for more information. Another cute place near by is the Bide-A-Wee Inn at 221 Asilomar Boulevard, down the street from Asilomar. This is an old world style place, oozing with charm, nestled behind the dunes, and a block or two from the water.

**Pacific Grove**

There's a boardwalk above the dunes at Asilomar State Beach, and you can walk over to Spanish Bay, past the golf course. Spanish Bay in on the 17 Mile drive, so you can walk or bike there for free, but driving will cost you $9.50 as of this writing, but that's subject to change. It's a lovely drive, but a better bike ride. Lots of mansions, upscale golf courses, beaches, the lone cypress, sea lions, etc. I've driven, biked and kayaked the area, and what blew me away was paddling over from Carmel, through Still Water

73

Cove and out around the point. Beyond the point, pushing through the thick kelp, I moved slowly along the shore and saw something you can't see from the road. There was a house, if you could call something that size a house. It was situated length wise along the shore, and it must have been a half block long. Off one end of the main, two-story house, was a tiny guesthouse, maybe 2000 square feet. These people owned almost a city block of some of the most expensive shoreline in the country, and the neighbor's house was almost as big.

This stretch of coast is also the location of a new big wave spot, called Ghost Tree. I've done some dumb things in the water, but riding 30 foot waves only a few yards from a boulder-strewn beach is far too crazy for me. However, if you are there in winter, you might see the most extreme surfing anywhere.

Monterey's northern limit bumps into three towns that seem to run together: Seaside, Sand City and Del Rey Oaks. Sand City has two good beach access places. One is at the foot of Canyon Del Rey Blvd., with a parking lot next to the Best Western Beach Resort. There's an exit off Highway One there. Just before entering the parking lot, you can also turn right on Sand Dunes Drive, which runs next to the freeway, and go a couple blocks to where it ends at Tioga Avene. Turn left and park. You now have access to miles of almost deserted beach, running along old Fort Ord and down to Marina. This is also a fairly good surfing spot.

After sunning, walking the beach or surfing, Go back on Tioga, turn right on California Avenue and then left on Hickory Street to the corner of Hickory and Ortiz Avenue, where you can find over 150 micro brews and sometimes live music at Post No Bills, a friendly place, filled with beer lovers.

Once you leave the Monterey Seaside and Sand City areas, you'll pass the old Fort Ord. There isn't much of the old military base left, a small administration community and a bunch of really old barracks that will probably be torn down one day soon to make room for development. I spent several months in basic training in one of those years ago, when I joined the National Guard.

California State University at Monterey Bay is now located there, along with some housing developments and some shopping. However, much of the land reverted to the Bureau of Land

Management, which means its public land, with trails and parking. The best spot is at the end of Reservation Road, a freeway exit in Marina. Just before Reservation crosses the 68 and becomes River Road, turn on Portola Drive and follow it up to the parking lot, complete with trail map and restrooms. Most of the trails work for hikers, bikers and equestrians. Also, from Highway One, enter the fort at Light Fighter Drive, right on Gen. Jim Moore and left on Giggling Road. Park at the end and hike or bike for miles.

We have another beach-goers treasure at Fort Ord, an almost natural, unspoiled and deserted beach. For decades the five mile stretch of beach along Fort Ord was closed, while trainees on the other side of the high dunes fired endlessly at paper targets. The rifle ranges are deserted now, and the beach, while closed from the highway, due to the dunes being filled with lead bullets, is open from both Marina and Sand City.

My curiosity about this stretch of beach dates back to when I was one of the trainees, awkwardly pointing a rifle toward the dunes. I finally satisfied that curiosity a few hours after the first rain of the season in the early 2000s. With a friend along, we parked one car in Sand City and drove the other to Marina, to the parking lot at the foot of Reservation Road.

Starting along the beach, we were struck by the size of the dunes. There is a vast ecosystem between the face of the dunes seen from the road and the beach, hills and valleys with scattered stands of native vegetation and nesting areas for birds. High above the town, these dunes offer a sweeping view of the Monterey Bay.

It was clear that this wasn't a typical beach. After walking a few yards, we had the beach to ourselves as far south as we could see. Also, looking up at the dunes, we quickly realized that there was almost no access. The dunes were so steep that any attempt to climb out would be like trying to climb to the roof of the gym on the stair step machine. In the entire five miles, there were two places low enough to climb, plus two gullies which the army had used for outflow pipes. These apparently lead back through the dunes and were perhaps made by seasonal creeks.

Big waves crashed against the shore, making it necessary for us to dash toward the dunes from time to time. Beyond the waves, dolphins and sea lions played, while groups of pelicans and gulls followed schools of fish.

On the beach, with no one to tidy up, there were the remains of dead seals, otters and gulls that had washed ashore. One carcass was surrounded by vultures, which retreated to their perches in the dunes as we passed. Odd pieces of flotsam and jetsam had found their way to the beach: old shoes, bottles, wads of fishing net and pieces of lumber.

We were almost constantly entertained by flocks of sanderlings and godwits as they rushed back and forth in their efforts to comb the beach for every morsel. On the sand or in the air, the flocks created artistic, flowing patterns of life.

The only impediment to our walk was Stilwell Hall, the old officers' club. In an effort to impede the inevitable retreat of the dunes, many tons of rocks were dumped below the structure, forcing us to climb along the rocks. Those rocks and Stillwell have now been claimed by the sea, the last of the rocks removed.

Stilwell Hall and the remains of two old outflow structures

 were the only signs of the previous rush of military activity. Other than that, we'd left civilization behind for three delightful hours.

Almost 45 years from the day I lay on the dunes with a rifle in my hands, I visited the **new park,** Almost dead center along that five-mile beach, and I was impressed. The parking lot is big enough to accommodate a moderate crowd, and there are **informational kiosks** that give directions, information and warnings about unleashed dogs. A 250-foot long wooden walkway leads to an overlook, where one can see miles of dunes and most of Monterey Bay.

While the ice plant, planted by the military, still dominates the dunes and can be quite beautiful in bloom, native wildflowers also dot the massive dunes; many so small they go unnoticed most of the year. However, in the spring, even the smallest erupts in splashes of pastel colors. Visitors can enjoy the dunes and their flowers from the trails, overlook and paved paths, but the dunes are not open to exploration, due to buried bullets and possible plover nests.

A 1500-foot trail leads down to the beach, starting with a paved road and becoming a sand path through the gully. Beach-combers, hikers, kite flyers and surfers were using the beach, and as I walked down the beach, the crowds thinned out, just as they had when I walked it a few years earlier.

Once away from the access gully, I found the sandpipers dancing on the beach. I didn't notice the vultures, which, I suppose, moved further down the beach to get away from the newly invasive creatures on their beach.

The beach is a little less wild than it once was, but it's more accessible for those who want to enjoy the beauty of nature, and all things considered, the state did an admirable job with our newest park. To get to the park, from Highway 1, exit Lightfighter Drive (bear right). Turn left onto 2nd Avenue. Turn left on 1st, 5th or 6th streets. Turn right on 1st Avenue. Signs posted will direct you to the park entrance at the 8th Street overcrossing of Hwy One.

Reservation Road ends at Marina State Beach, with a parking lot, rest rooms, miles of beach and a launch ramp for hang gliders. It's very popular with hang gliders in the afternoon, when the wind comes up. The usual pattern is surfers and beach walkers in the morning, gliders in the afternoon. The waves are usually good, and in the winter can be huge and intimidating. If you don't want to go in the water or go hang gliding, there's a trail through the dunes that will give you a brief overview of the local ecology. There has been a big effort to restore native plants on these dunes. There are a couple of motels in the immediate area, and it's a good spot to park for a bike ride along the path through Fort Ord to Sea-side, about five miles each way, and there are no cars. I love doing this, and at the other end, I grab a coffee, relax in the cool breeze and then head back.

For a serious bike rider who is vacationing in the Monterey area, here's the long and scenic route. North of Marina, at the last exit before the freeway becomes a two lane road, Nashua/Molera Roads. Go right on Nashua a short block to Del Monte, and find a place to park. The bike path runs along Del Monte through Marina, where it enters Fort Ord. There are two paths, one between the fence and the freeway, and the other on the ocean side of the fence, an old road. Once the path exits Fort Ord, there's a big shopping center, and the path turns up the dunes and then back down behind one end of the shopping center, going for a block behind the buildings. Then it turns for a block shoreward on Tioga. Then the separate path starts again, running behind the beach down by the Best Western Beach Resort, a great place to stay if you want to be on the beach. The path keeps going either up the dunes or on the other side of the freeway, along the lagoon. Then it follows Del Monte Blvd. to the Plaza and Fisherman's Wharf and on to Cannery Row, continuing out to Lovers Point Park, where it becomes a bike lane along the road next to the beach and around the point. Then as you go up and away from the beach, turn right on 17 Mile Drive and go through Pebble Beach to Carmel. Altogether, it's about 25-30 miles of the most scenic bike paths I've seen.

Once driving north out of Marina, be careful of your speed. The freeway that ends and becomes a two lane road near Castroville is a speed trap. Straight, uncrowded roads lull one into letting the speed gradually climb, and I've seen as many as six cars pulled over at the same time on a four mile stretch. 65 means 64, so be warned.

Don't stop in Castroville. It's a little residential town, and

there isn't much for the traveler except for the Giant Artichoke restaurant and the very small annual Artichoke Festival. You will see a sign; ignore it and drive a couple more miles to **Moss Landing,** a small harbor town with at least as much charm per block as San Francisco or New York. I drive to Moss Landing three to four times a week, ostensibly to check the surf, but mostly

78

just because it's there.

As you approach town, you'll see a liquor store on the left, you can turn there and either drive toward the beach, where surfers, walkers and horseback riders share the beach, or follow Moss Landing Road, which almost parallels the highway. Or if you stay on the highway, the next left is just past the Whole Enchilada Restaurant, which serves decent Mexican food and has a full bar. Next door is the Lighthouse Harbor Grille, a place that serves a very ample and delicious breakfast. A more interesting but expensive alternative to the Whole Enchilada is the Haute Enchilada on Moss Landing Road.

Moss Landing is beach, antique shops, marine research facilities, great surf and wonderful seafood. It's also a fishing harbor and a wildlife wonderland. There's also a B and B on Moss Land-

ing Road, if you have a mind to spend the night.

As you drive down Moss Landing Road, you'll find Sandholdt Road going over a bridge to the "island," which isn't strictly an island, but that's not important. Just over the bridge, to the left is a parking lot for a great beach, a popular spot for board and **kayak surfers**. However, staying on the road you'll pass the research institute associated with the Monterey Bay Aquarium, and they occasionally have an open house for the public. Just past that is Phil's Seafood Restaurant and Fish Market, a landmark, a great place to eat, a place where everyone from a hundred mile radius stops by from time to time, and the home of some of the best Manhattan style clam chowder on the coast.

A couple of blocks past Phil's the road ends at the jetty, a popular place for fishermen. Once you go back over the bridge, stop at the fruit and veggie market or at the biker bar next door to the Whole Enchilada. Then turn left and go over the entrance to Elkhorn Slough, and turn left again into the next parking lot. Now, this is the most important parking lot along the Monterey Bay, so

I'll take a bit of time with it.

On the south end of the lot is another Sea Harvest Restaurant—remember the Crossroads Shopping Center in Carmel? This is my favorite restaurant this side of Tuscany, Italy. What can I say: Great fresh fish, al dente veggies, wine glass filled to the top and moderate prices. I've never had a meal there that I would rate fewer than five stars.

This parking lot serves the harbor and boat docks. At the other end of the lot is a pottery store and Monterey Bay Kayaks. Yes, you can rent kayaks here or take a tour. Also, on the other side of the fence at the north end of the lot, you'll find Kayak Connection. Mark, the former owner is an avid kayak surfer and stand up paddler. The new owners are Dave and Jessica Grigsby.

So, you are saying, "I'm on a vacation; why in the world would I want to stop to rent a kayak?" My answer is that you'll see more wildlife in a three hour paddle in the slough than any other place on the west coast. Let's see: otters, up close and personal, sea lions, seals, gulls, pelicans, terns,  herons, egrets, sand pipers, plovers, etc, and all in abundance. **The Slough** is basically calm and flat unless it's really windy. Take the tour, and let the pros show you around. I can almost guarantee you'll have a great time. I've paddled this almost a hundred times, and I'm never bored.

Just before the bridge that takes you to the island, there's the entrance to the harbor, and just inside is another whale watching boat, Sanctuary Cruises, another place to go whale watching. I liked the former owners, but haven't met the new ones.

Notice that when you in the parking lot in front of Monterey Bay Kayaks or at the Sea Harvest, look toward the ocean, and you'll see, in the harbor, dozens of sea otters. If you have a zoom on your camera, you can get some great close ups of them playing in the water. Get a preview at http://www.youtube.com/watch?v=tp6Sg3CZm9U.

If you want to stay in the area and not in a motel or B and B, go a mile back south to Molera Road, and head toward the beach. Monterey Dunes (http://www.montereydunes.com/index.htm) has rentals right on the beach.

Hopefully you've had the time of your life in Moss Landing, eaten some fresh fish and maybe even picked up an antique lamp. Now, as you start to head north, you'll see, on the left, J & S Surplus. This place has been there nearly forever, and you can even buy an old army jeep. However, if you are camping, they have something that costs perhaps a buck and is the camper's best friend, a P-38. This is a tiny, folding can opener, no more than an inch long and less than a centimeter thick, and it will open any can with only a minute's effort.

J & S is on the corner of Struve Road, where you can access Zmudowski State Beach, a long and underused stretch of sand. You will make a series of lefts and rights, always headed toward the water, for about two miles. From here, you can walk the beach back to Moss Landing or north to the mouth of the Pajaro River. But be warned. It's an isolated beach, and auto thefts do happen, so don't leave your valuables in the car.

About three miles up the road, the freeway starts again, and you cross into Santa Cruz County. The first town you come to is Watsonville, known as the Strawberry Capital, and they don't want to hear about the great berries you bought in Oceano. There isn't much worth stopping for here, unless you enjoy walking

along wetlands and/or you are a birder. The **Watsonville Slough system,** easily accessed from the freeway is a birder's paradise, and the city

81

has built several miles of walking trails along the sloughs. They now have an annual birding festival in late summer or early fall. If you have time to stop, here is a map of the trail system: http://www.watsonvilleslough.org/trailmap1.pdf.

If you are a birder and want to hang out for a day, the Red Roof Inn is located just off the 129 (Riverside Drive) exit, and at the next exit is a Motel 6. There's a little shopping center near the sloughs, but don't bother going downtown, as it is drying up, with many vacant storefronts.

From the Red Roof Inn, heading away from Riverside, there's a stop sign at Beach Street. Turn left and go three miles to another stretch of beach. Parking is on the north side of Beach, and Pajaro Dunes is on the south. Pajaro Dunes has summer rentals, and it's a closed community, so if you want to beach in style, check out http://www.pajarodunesvacation.com/?gclid=CLbw7bz3yqsCFRdl gwod_n0T4Q.

Once past Watsonville, you go from a working class town to an affluent community, Aptos. If you exit San Andreas Road, and go toward the beach, you'll come to a stop sign at Seascape Blvd. Turn right and go to the end and you'll drive right into the Seascape Resort. This is nice, located right on the coast and would be a great base of operations for anyone visiting the area. Sander-lings Restaurant has outstanding food, and the windows face the sunset over the ocean. Talk about a romantic setting. But wait, there's more. They have weeknight dinner specials. http://www.seascaperesort.com/.

But, before settling in for the night and having a great meal, you want to get out of the car and either take a hike or a mountain bike ride. Naturally. Well, The Forest of Nisene Marks is the place. It's located off Soquel Drive between the Rio Del Mar and State Park exits. You want Aptos Creek Road in Aptos Village. Drive in and park. There are miles of trails along the creek and through the redwoods. The road becomes a dirt road, which eventually be-comes a fire road, and you can ride your bike through the park, be-yond where it's closed to cars. About five miles in, you hit a section called The Incline, and yes, it is aptly named. Then it levels out just a wee bit and continues to the Sand Point Overlook, a destination that will make you feel good about yourself. But if you are macho, you can continue on the uphill to the top of the park, another really steep section.

While I don't recommend it because of the logistics of getting back, I remember having fun continuing north from the top past Buzzard Lagoon and down Buzzard Lagoon Road, a white knuckle downhill that puts you several miles south of where you left the car.

Did that ride or hike make you thirsty? Note that when you turned up Aptos Creek Road, there was a Britannia Arms on Soquel. What can I say, except that they have good pub food and a large selection of ales. But, if you don't like pub food, drive a bit further up Soquel, past State Park Drive and look for a small shopping center on the left. You'll find Zameen's Mediterranean Cuisine at 7528 Soquel Dr. I'm a nut for falafels, and I've eaten them everywhere. Zameen's has probably the best and certainly the biggest I've ever had.

If you'd rather have Indian food, take State Park over the freeway to 207 Sea Ridge Rd, just to the right, to Ambrosia India Bistro, which just happens to have a lunch buffet.

There is also a place to stay in the area, also with a good restaurant, the Best Western Seacliff Inn right off the corner of Soquel and State Park, on Old Dominion Ct., a side road off State Park. Nice accommodations and the restaurant is Severino's, which has nightly early bird specials and a nice happy hour, plus live music.

Before we get too far into Santa Cruz County, it's time to discuss some beach camping options. Two of these are off San Andreas Road, which you can access at the first Santa Cruz County off ramp, Riverside Drive (Hwy 129), by going left, then right at the end and left again at the light. San Andreas Rd. will be the first right, 2 miles west. Or San Andreas Road is a freeway exit several miles north. It's the one that leads to Seascape Resort. The two campgrounds are Sunset State Beach (see the sign on San Andreas Rd.) and Manresa State Beach. There are two Manresas, the parking lot for day use and the Uplands camping area, which has walk in campsites only. Both of these allow you to camp on the coast and walk down to the beach. Both, due to state funding limitations, are open only during the summer months, and both are subject to filling up, so it might be wise to make reservations.

The other two are Seacliff State Beach and New Brighton State Beach. Seacliff is located at the end of State Park Drive, and it's an RV only place, a long paved stretch on the beach. For New Brighton, take the next exit going north, Park Avenue Turn left, and it's just past the frontage road. We'll look at the mountain camping areas in a bit.

Capitola and Soquel are the next communities, Capitola being the town on the ocean side of the freeway. Exit 41st Avenue, headed for the beach. There's a mall on 41st, the only actual enclosed mall in the county. I'm not suggesting you shop, but if you

 need something, it's right there. If you continue to the end of the road it hits the beach at a famous surfing area called

**Pleasure Point**. Actually the road along the point is one way from the other way, but there's a parking lot at the end of 41st, and you can walk along and check out the waves. Also, across Capitola Road from the mall is one of the better of the remaining independent book stores, Capitola Book Cafe. Many well-known writers have done talks and book signings there, usually on Tuesday night, so if you're in the area, stop by. Also, Inklings Book Store is located inside the mall.

Since you can't turn right at the end of 41st, turn left and in about a mile you'll drop down the hill into Capitola Village, a really cute beach community, complete with pier, bars, restaurants, places to stay, gift shops and all things you might associate with the beach. There are lots of beach rental houses on or near the village, and there are real estate businesses which specialize in renting these, so if you want to spend a week or two in style, put

84

"Capitola summer rentals" in your browser. If you don't live on the coast, you can easily spend a summer week in **Capitola.** Also, during the sum-

mer they have free concerts on the beach on Wednesday evenings.

Santa Cruz, to avoid confusion, can be divided into three tourist compartments: The beach, the downtown, and the mountains. We'll start with the easiest, the beach. If you exit Ocean Street at the end of the freeway, where the road curves around, you will be heading toward the beach. At Broadway, turn right and go over the river. Broadway becomes Laurel, and turn left at the light at Center Street. That will take you right down to the Wharf. You can drive out on the wharf, and there are restaurants, bars, gift shops, ice cream and chocolate and fishing. Gilda's Restaurant has

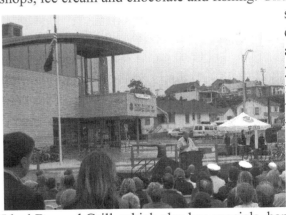

some weekday specials that are good and priced to get your attention. But for fancier fare, go to one of the next three or four eateries.

Right on the corner at the foot of the wharf is the Ideal Bar and Grill, which also has specials, happy hours and a young party atmosphere. I recommend it to traveling singles, but line up one of the local motels first, as you may not be in condition to drive after an evening there.

A new addition to the area around the wharf and Boardwalk is the Monterey Bay **National Marine Sanctuary Visitors Center,**

85

just up the street from the wharf. It opened in the summer of 2012, and I encourage anyone visiting the area to check it out. They have some informative exhibits and a great film about the sanctuary.

Turning left there, at Beach Street, you find the Boardwalk. This is one of the last big beach boardwalk amusement parks left on the West Coast. It's open every day and night in summer, but has limited hours the rest of the year. Unlike others that are dying out, this one is growing and still very popular. In the summer they have free Friday night concerts, mainly groups that were really big some years back, but who still can give a rousing performance.

In front of the Boardwalk is Main Beach, a place to spend the day with the kids. There are motels across from the Boardwalk, up on Beach Hill. The ones down on the flats are pretty seedy, so definitely go up the hill, which is between the Boardwalk and the Wharf and up from Beach Street.

However, once down at the beach and looking at the Wharf, you can also turn right and go up a short hill. That will take you to West Cliff Drive. Note the hotel, the Dream Inn, at the top of the hill. Good views and a popular place. It sits right above Cowell's Beach, one of the best beginner surfing spots on the coast. If you continue past Cowell's and the Dream Inn for about a half-mile, you reach the lighthouse, now the home of the Surfing Museum. The surf break below the museum is Steamer Lane at Lighthouse Field, one of the best, and not for beginners, breaks on the coast. You can stand at the rail and watch some of the most impressive surfing, or you can suit up and give it a shot. Each spring, there's a big kayak surfing contest there, fun to watch, fun to compete in.

West Cliff runs along the bluffs, and there's a biking, running, walking trail, which ends at Natural Bridges State Park, about a three mile stretch. And beyond that, you start to exit Santa Cruz and enter the north coast. Natural Bridges has a small forest that attracts the yearly migration of Monarch butterflies. Celebrate the butterflies' arrival with the Welcome Back Monarchs Day in October - and their departure with the Migration Festival in February. However, you can't camp there.

Downtown Santa Cruz is mostly Pacific Avenue, the streets on either side and the cross streets. If you come back from the beach on Center, make a right and a left at the next light, you'll be on Pacific. Just park someplace. This is also called the **Pacific Garden Mall**, and it's a walking place. People wander around,

 shopping, eating, drinking, listening to street musicians, chatting and just hanging out. It's a good downtown, if you don't mind the odd panhandler. You can buy a meal, a drink, a book, art, jewelry, coffee, candy and even a new surfboard. There are even wine bars, but these days, there are always wine bars. If you like beer, 99 Bottles, just off Pacific, has good food and, well, 99 different beers and ales. Also, another excellent independent bookstore, Bookshop Santa Cruz is on Pacific Avenue. Large and very complete, it has weathered earthquakes and major competition, and it's still going strong.

There are other sections of town worth visiting, but best get your basic tourist info if you plan to do more than stop on your way.

The Santa Cruz Mountains start on the inland side of Highway One. When you come off the freeway at Ocean, take the first right, go by the front of Denny's restaurant and up Graham Hill Road. A few miles up the road you'll see the entrance to Henry Cowell State Park campground, another place that fills up quickly. Pass that, and you'll come to Roaring Camp Railroad, where you can take an old fashioned logging train ride through the redwoods. Then continue up Graham Hill and you'll enter the charming little mountain town of Felton. If you turn left at the light at Highway 9, you'll be headed toward the day use area of Henry Cowell State Park. They have a paved walk, about a mile or so, through a wonderful old growth redwood forest, plus many miles of other hiking trails, some down to swimming holes on the San Lorenzo River.

If you don't turn left on 9, you can either go straight, past the excellent Hallcrest Vinyards, an organic winery on the left to the parking lot for the Fall Creek part of Cowell Park, where you can hike along the creek through more redwoods.

The other choice is to go right on Highway 9, up through the woods to Boulder Creek is the last town along the road until you go down into the Santa Clara Valley, miles away. They have a brew pub downtown, and I suggest a stop. Then make a left on Big Basin Way and drive the nine miles to Big Basin State Park, with its miles of trails. Ask the ranger about the trail to the falls, four miles each way, and well worth the walk. Big Basin offers day use and camping, and that pretty much exhausts the public camping. There are, however, private camp and RV parks in the area.

Back on Highway One, the freeway becomes Mission Street, with signals, businesses and all that. Near the end of Mission, and just off it on the ocean side, at Fair Avenue is the Franz Lanting Gallery. Lanting is a world class nature photographer, and his huge prints will hold you spell bound. Also, between Fair and Swift, along Ingalls Street, is a little shopping center, with two wineries, the Santa Cruz Brewing Company and Kelly's Bakery. The wines are good, but Kelly's baked goods and the brewery's ales are something to write home about.

Once past Swift Street, you quickly exit Santa Cruz and enter the North Coast.

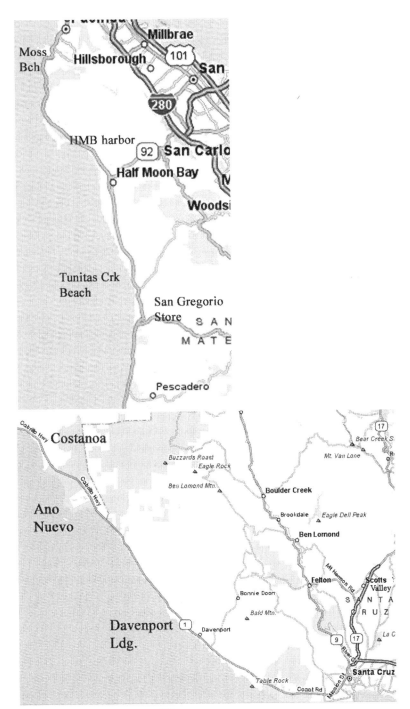

# From Santa Cruz to Pacifica

Before you leave town, turn left off Mission on Swift, then right on Delaware.

You'll drive past Natural Bridges, so if you haven't stopped, do so. But, keep going to the end of the road to the Seymour Center at Long Marine Laboratory. It's informative, rather like a mini version of the aquarium in Monterey.

As you drive down Mission Street and past the last light at Western Drive, you enter a section of coast that includes the Santa Cruz north coast and the San Mateo Coast. This, mostly open, scenic area hosts many popular recreation destinations, including state beaches and hidden coves. Development pressures threatened much of this area, but environmental activists in both counties formed organizations and managed to preserve much

of it. For example, Gray Whale Ranch, abutting **Wilder Ranch State Park** was involved in a big tug of war, and now the area, reaching almost to the coast and connecting with UC Santa Cruz is parkland, offering rolling hills, streams and groves of redwoods.

Coast Dairies, a bit further north, was scheduled for various kinds of development in the late 90s, and activist organizations were trying to acquire it and were picketing to raise local awareness. In fact one activist meeting was interrupted by the news that a deal was made. The would-be picketers drank copious amounts of wine, turned their picket signs into fire wood and went home.

Within a mile of leaving Santa Cruz, you see a sign for Wilder Ranch. You can drive in to visit the historic buildings on the coast side and wander the trails down to the bluffs. It's a great old ranch and well preserved. However, most people pull over on the ocean side of the road, where there is ample parking, and either mountain bike or hike on the inland side. There are several miles of multi-use trails, but hikers need to take care, as there are many bikes on the weekend, and they're usually out to burn up the trails. Be ready to hop off the trail, but if you are a mountain biker, Wilder and Gray Whale offer steep climbs, white knuckle down hills, single track, fire roads and even creek crossings. You can easily spend a day or a weekend there.

At some point Wilder sort of fades into Coast Dairies, but that property isn't marked. You just find lots of open land, and there are trails leading down to the bluffs and beaches. There are some popular surf spots in this stretch. There is room for a few cars at Three Mile, named because it's three miles from town. You walk a trail to the bluff and then down the bluff to the beach. There's a big dirt parking area at Four Mile. Four Mile has a great beach, so it's not just for the surfers who enjoy the usually excellent right break. It's about a five to ten minute walk down to the beach, and there are even some porta potties just before you reach the beach.

There's another nice little beach across from Bonny Doon Road, about ten miles from Santa Cruz, and there's plenty of parking along the highway. You can also drive four miles up Bonny Doon Road to the outskirts of Bonny Doon, which isn't really a town, but at that first intersection, there's a great little winery with

 lots of wines to sample.

At eleven miles from

Santa Cruz, slow down, as the speed limit drops to 45 as you enter **Davenport**, a wide spot along the road. Not only is there a speed limit, but people are   always crossing the road, to get from the restaurants and bars to the beach and back.

Davenport is a popular place to stop, or as a destination on a nice day. It's particularly popular with motorcyclists, who cruise the highway and the winding roads that snake back into the redwood canyons. Bonny Doon and Pescadero, a

Davenport Landing

little further north, are great motorcycle and bicycle areas, the roads just too inviting to pass up, and you always manage to pass through Davenport on the way back to town.

Once, when I didn't know the back roads all that well, I rode my motorcycle down from Pacifica and started to wander the roads around Bonny Doon. I'm still not sure what road I ended up on, and I haven't found it since, but I came to a dead end at some youth camp, and the bike died. There was no one for miles to give me a hand, and if I hadn't been on a slight hill, I would have had to walk for hours to civilization. The Santa Cruz mountains can be remote.

The most popular place to stop is the Whale City Bakery, Bar and Grill. They have coffee, beer, food, outside and inside tables, and one of the best atmospheres for chatting with perfect strangers on any of the 300 perfect days they have each year. It's a popular stop for hikers, bicyclists and motorcyclists. And, if you are into real dining and perhaps staying the night, the Davenport Roadhouse is also there. It's all easy to find, as the town is two blocks wide and two deep. There's also Arro's store and the art gallery. Do visit the art gallery. I won't tell you what delights you'll find there, as it's a cooperative, and things change from month to month.

Across from the town there are hiking trails along the bluffs and even some trails down to    little coves.

Just past the town, after the 45 limit ends, you can turn left to Davenport Landing. It's one way, with the road coming back to the highway about a half mile north.

There are a few homes there, along with a public beach, which even has restrooms. As you pass the restrooms and look at the beach, you'll see two areas with waves. On the left a shallow reef sticks out, and off the end of the reef is a good surf break, usually with several people in the water. The right side of the beach ends at rocky bluffs that extend out quite a way. This side also has waves, but is often surfed by kayaks. I remember a kayak surf gathering in six to eight foot surf. The almost perfect waves ended in the deep channel in the middle of the small bay, so getting out of the wave and back out was easy, if you didn't get caught inside and shoved into the rocks. When it gets big enough to break across the entire bay, only the seriously brave and possibly insane go out.

At the north end of the beach, a trail goes up the bluff, and in the spring you can walk a mile or more through waist-high wildflowers.

There are a few more beaches you can pull off and enjoy, such as the beach at **Scott Creek**, another popular sunbathing and surfing spot. Also, look for the fruit and veggie stands along that stretch of highway, particularly in the spring and summer. Swanton Berry Farm has stand, but further up the road they also offer a "You Pick" option. Naturally, this is only in the spring and summer.

Also, for a scenic alternative route for either driving or biking, opposite from the Davenport landing road exit there is Swanton Road, which ends up back on Highway One by Greyhound Rock, after wandering about seven miles through some lovely country and lush redwoods on the way. It passes by Big Creek Lumber and Swanton Pacific Railway, a scaled down version of a railroad, owned by Cal Poly University.

Either Highway One or Swanton Road will get you to Greyhound Rock County Park, which has a parking lot, restrooms and a steep, paved trail way down to the beach, with a hand rail near the bottom. The park is named for the huge rock just off the surf line, reachable at low tide. It's a great beach, and sometimes even a surfing spot. It's also a good beach for wandering and looking for tide pools and shore birds.

Just north of Greyhound Rock is the Waddell Creek and beach area, but before going down the hill to beach level, there's a turnout on the ocean side with room for a half dozen cars. A trail runs down the bluff to the beach and the rock reefs that extend out, making it a great place for surfing or tide pooling at low tide. The top of the bluff is a great place to sit in the ice plant, dangle your feet over the edge and watch the sunset, particularly on a cloudy day. I saw one of the best sunsets one Halloween, and just as the sun dropped below the horizon, a jet out of San Francisco left a glowing trail across the sky. As I turned back to the car, the hillside was glowing in the orange of the dying light.

Down at the bottom of the hill is **Waddell Creek and beach**. There's a dirt parking lot, which is popular with surfers in the morning and wind and kite surfers in the afternoon, and you'll get a spectacular show almost any afternoon. Across from the parking lot there's a trail, a dirt road, actually, that runs along Waddell Creek and is part of Big Basin State Park. The best way to see this area is to pullout your mountain bike and ride the five miles to where the dirt road ends. There's a bike rack there, and then you have to cross the creek and take a foot trail another

94

almost half mile to Berry Creek Falls, one of the prettiest water-falls in the Santa Cruz Mountains. If you don't have a bike with you, you can hike the whole thing, but that's eleven miles and most of a day. With the exception of the first part of this road, serving a few local ranches, there are no motorized vehicles, so biking along the creek and under the redwoods is a relaxing pleasure. Some people start at the park's main entrance above Boulder Creek and hike down to the falls, four miles and then down to the beach. The bus back to town isn't running, so plan a car shuttle.

This is one of most pleasant areas I've biked. The creek bottom sparkles golden in the clear stream, and the redwoods alternate with a mixed forest. There are a couple of places where the old road is almost gone, becoming a single track, and even requiring getting off the bike. Once at the bike rack, it's only a few minutes through the forest to the base of the falls, and there's a platform where you can sit and take photos. You can also hike to the top and further up the hill to two more smaller falls.

While you are standing there, deciding whether to go to the beach or up Waddell Creek, look up at Waddell Bluffs. See how these go straight up? These kept a road from Santa Cruz to San Francisco from going through for many years. Earlier travelers had to walk or ride their horses along the beach, and at higher tides, that meant waves slamming them into the cliffs.

Once past the bluffs, you exit Santa Cruz County and enter San Mateo County, and as you go back up the hill, you'll see the Coastways Ranch driveway on the right. Just south of that and on the ocean side is a trail down to Bradley Beach, a very secluded place, with a sheltered cove piece of beach. You'll walk around a closed gate and thus cross private property, so be respectful and pack your trash. We want the owners to keep it open.

A half mile north is Ano Nuevo State Park. This is another place you can view elephant seals, watch the big males sparring for females and mothers nursing their young, but the public flow is controlled and limited, so check with them first. There's no camping, but there are miles of trail along the coast, from the main part of the park, through a maze of wildflower-covered dunes, down to Gazos Creek State Beach, which has parking, restrooms and picnic facilities. You have to walk quite a ways from the parking lot to the beach where the elephant seals hang out, and when you get there, look over the narrow channel at the island with the old building. Once people left the island, the sea lions took over, and now that building is filled with some very smelly and loud marine mammals.

You can also drive up Gazos Creek Road a short way to Butano State Park. This in another great redwood-forested park, and there are trails along the creek and up through the woods. There are trails that connect Butano to other parks, all the way up to Highway 35, on the spine between the coast and the Silicon Valley. You could spend days up there, as there is a chain of at least a dozen state and county parks.

At Gazos Creek, there is a gas station and restaurant combination. I don't know about the other meals, but I recall breakfast being pretty good. There isn't much else along the highway until almost Half Moon Bay.

You might want to spend some time in the area, so just a couple miles north, at Rossi Road, you'll see the sign for Costanoa Resort and Campground. You can fancy it up at the resort or camp in their campground, and I hear the restaurant is very good. Staying there, the only resort in the area, gives you access to hundreds of miles of trails and several state parks. It's all wide open coastal country, not a traffic signal or high rise city building for many miles. You can get more info at: http://www.costanoa.com/site.php

Drive up Whitehouse Road, just south of Rossi Rd., and as you get into the canyon, there are trails up through the woods, meeting up with mountain bike routes, which can take you through the state wilderness to Big Basin. Those hills are simply full of trails. If you stay at Costanoa, you can keep yourself busy for days.

A few short miles north is **Pigeon Point Lighthouse** and Hostel. The lighthouse was closed but might be open by the time you visit. The hostel is open; accommodations are in shared, gender-specific

dorm rooms, or in private rooms. Bathrooms are shared. Choices are: shared dorm rooms (6 beds per room), private single/double room or private family room. The hostel offers several areas for guests to relax and enjoy, including: Comfortable lounges with board games and library, outdoor patio with picnic tables and barbecue, cliff top hot tub, historic fog signal building with wood stove, oceanfront boardwalk and walking trail and beach access. The hostel has three self-service kitchens where you can prepare your meals. All that you need to prepare a meal is provided.

Also, just south of the lighthouse, there are dirt roads leading down to the bluffs, and there are new steps leading down to the beach. If you are self-contained, you can probably spend the night on the bluffs, but I don't think it qualifies as official camping. Then again, I've spent hundreds of nights on non-official camping place, often my more peaceful night's rests.

Walk around the area around the lighthouse, and check out the rocky shore. It's a good place to take some photos.

Bean Hollow is the next spot, a small cove with a beach, parking and some outhouses. This is where Bean Hollow Road cuts off, and if you take it, you will wind through some magnificent coastal hills until you hit Pescadero Creek Road, where you can go right a mile to the town of Pescadero or left a mile to Highway One.

But, let's go back to Bean Hollow Beach. If you stay on Highway One, you'll pass a few homes along the water and some farms or ranches inland—the quiet, country life. Then you'll come to Pescadero State Beach, with the dramatic, rocky shoreline, parking, restrooms and the Pescadero Marsh on the inland side. This is where Pescadero Creek road heads inland to Pescadero and beyond, to Memorial County Park, Sam McDonald County Park and all the way up to Highway 84 in La Honda, which I'll mention again in just a bit.

Pescadero is the only thing resembling a town in the area, a few blocks of buildings and homes. There are a couple places to eat and drink that are popular with the pedal bikers and motorcycle bikers. Duarte's Tavern is famous for its pies, soup and cioppino. Just drive into town and see where the cars and bikes are parked.

The main intersection in town is at Stage Road, and if you

are into bike riding, the ride between Pescadero and San Gregorio is an exceptional 14 mile round trip. I did it from San Gregorio, and from there the road climbs and climbs and climbs. Then it drops steeply, which made me happy until I realized that it climbs and climbs steeply one last time before it crests the hill. At the top, there are great views of the coast, and I recall a stand of flowers with a bunch of bumble bees flying around, something to watch and enjoy while trying to catch my breath before the long down hill. At the bottom of the hill, the road wanders through charming ranches and farms before reaching Pescadero. The ride back is a bit easier, as the uphill is more gradual.

The other way to get to San Gregorio is to go back to Highway One, and continue to Pomponio State Beach, another place with coastal access, parking, restrooms and picnic areas, and then on to San Gregorio State Beach, which is a lot like Pomponio, a lovely beach where a creek meets the ocean. In between, the road climbs high along the bluffs, making beach access difficult or impossible.

At San Gregorio State Beach, Highway one intersects Highway 84. You'll want to turn there and go the mile to the **San Gregorio Store**. It's a very cool old store (since 1889), with books, clothes, hats, various and sundry general store items, a bar with food, and on the weekends they often have a local band. This is a throwback to the days when small towns really had general stores, where people picked up the things they needed and talked with neighbors before heading back to the farm.

The owner, George, who taught at Stanford University for ten years, is a strong environmentalist and political activist and has brought that sensibility to his store, which probably didn't look much different at the turn of the twentieth century. You'll find a wide selection of poetry, music and literature. And, if you stop for a beer, you're almost certain to find a character to pass the time with, perhaps even George, himself.

If you continue up 84 another seven miles, you'll find the community, I can't really say town, of La Honda. It may not ring a bell, but think of Ken Kesey and the Merry Pranksters. This is where they hung out, along with the Hell's Angels, during the sixties. There is funky little bar in the redwoods, right off the high-way, that reeks with local flavor. But not too many beers, as Highway One still calls. **Tunitas Creek** Road is another road that goes all the way to the 35 (Skyline). You can bike that, or you can pull off in the dirt, along the bluffs just south of the creek and road. There are trails leading down to the **beach**, a wonderful beach, with scenic bluffs jutting straight up on the north side of the creek.

Continuing further north, you'll see Martin's Beach, which used to be open to the public for a fee. The pressure is on the new owner to open it up again, so it's hard to say what will happen. It's been in the news as I write this, and people have been coming forward to talk about how they've been going there for two or three generations. It's a surf spot, a sunbathing and picnicking spot, a family outing spot and even the scene of many weddings. It's too much a part of the extended community to be lost behind a locked gate.

Just a bit further Verde Road goes off to the right. It connects with Purisima Creek Road, and if you drive about fifteen minutes up that road, you'll run right into Purisima Creek Redwoods Open Space, which is worth spending a few hours exploring. There are some great hiking trails, and the main trail/fire road is a super bike ride to the top, Skyline Drive (Hwy 35). But, be warned, that last section feels like riding up the side of the Empire State Building. Once on top you can come back down the same way or go south to either Tunitas Creek Road or further to Hwy 84 back to Highway One.

Also, at the park, the road makes a hairpin turn back toward the coast, so you can either go back the way you came or continue on Higgins Canyon Road to the city of Half Moon Bay. But if you turn around and go back to the highway and turn north, as you approach Half Moon Bay, there is, on the right, the ultimate spring and summer **fruit and veggie stand.** See the sign that says "Peas, no spray." If you've never eaten fresh, super sweet peas right from the pod, this is your chance to experience a true delight. I always buy a pound, which are finished by the time I hit Pacifica. They also have a wide assortment of other fruits and veggies.

Half Moon Bay is a growing community. The population was about 7,000 when I lived in the area, and I think it's somewhere around now 13,000. Had the developers and Cal Trans gotten their way and a massive freeway put in from Pacifica, the population would probably be several times larger. Half Moon Bay and Pacifica are the only real cities along this stretch of coast.

As you enter town, Main Street angles off to the right. That's the downtown area, with all the little shops that you expect to find on Main Street. Main ends at Highway 92, which winds up over the hill, intersects with Highway 280 and continues as a freeway into San Mateo and over the San Mateo Bridge to Hayward in the East Bay.

There are many places to stay in town, along with an RV park on Highway One and several bed and breakfasts. There are also many restaurants, but I can't think of one that stands out in my mind, but north in Princeton, which adjoins Half Moon Bay, there are a couple I would recommend.

As you drive through town, there are art galleries, a wood craft store, a market, coffee shops and a couple of delightful little bookstores, and with the independents closing almost daily, who knows how long they'll be around.

If you are there in October, the town has a pumpkin festival which is one of the better street festivals on the coast, which is saying a lot, due to the fact that most towns seem to have one.

Venice Beach Blvd. will take you down to the main beach, which has a bike and walking trail just in from the beach and which runs along the water through town.

On the north end, Half Moon Bay bleeds into the community of Miramar, where you'll see a sign for the Miramar Beach Inn, an old and well known restaurant and bar, just off the highway, near the water.

As you start to exit town, the highway will run along the beach for a short way, and you'll probably see surfers playing in the small waves. You'll also see a jetty at the end of that beach, and that marks the Half Moon Bay harbor. Then you'll come to a signal, Capistrano Road. Turn left, and you're in **Princeton-by-the-Sea.**

In a short block you'll see Barbara's Fish Trap on the left, a great place for sea food, and on the right the Half Moon Bay Brewing Company. They have a great selection of hand-crafted ales and a full menu. You can have a cold pint (I love their IPA) and watch videos of people riding the big waves at Mavericks, out beyond the harbor.

If it's winter and there's a big swell, you can watch these very scary waves break by turning left on Prospect Way, left on Harvard and right on West Point Avenue There's a parking lot at the end, and then you walk several blocks to the beach, where the outer breakwater meets the point. The big surf breaks out past that jumble of very mean rocks off the beach. Bring binoculars, as the waves are way off shore.

Princeton is a good place to hang out. If you have your kayak, you can launch in the harbor and paddle around in calm water before venturing out into the open ocean. If you want to spend the night, there's the Maverick's Lodge and Event Center, right down by the water, just a couple blocks from the brewery.

If you didn't bring a kayak but want to explore the harbor, you can rent or take a tour: http://www.hmbkayak.com/home.html

Once you leave Princeton, you're about twenty miles from San Francisco. But first you'll go through two small beach towns, Moss Beach and Montara. Moss Beach has -two things worth stopping for. **Fitzgerald Marine Reserve**, a three-mile long tide

 pooler's paradise. If you like poking around in the tide pools and

looking at all the wonderful creatures among the rocks, turn left on either Virginia or California Avenues and drive to the water, but this is a county reserve, so don't disturb anything living.

If you'd rather just eat and drink, watch for the signs to the Moss Beach Distillery. This restaurant and bar, right on the water is famous for their supposed ghost. You are unlikely to see the ghost, but you'll find a full menu of spirits, plus excellent meals, and you can watch the sunset from the deck.

Montara is next, but there isn't much there beside a long, sandy beach, good for walking and surfing. There are a couple of restaurants along the highway that are worth stopping at, as well as some bed and breakfast places. Plus there's the **Point Montara Lighthouse Hostel**. It's a lighthouse; it's a hostel. It's actually both, and it is quite popular.

Once you pass Montara and the long, wide beach, you start

102

 to rise up toward Devil's Slide. You'll see where they are building the tunnel that will bypass the slide, which everyone hopes won't crumble into the sea before it's finished. On the other side of the slide is Pacifica.

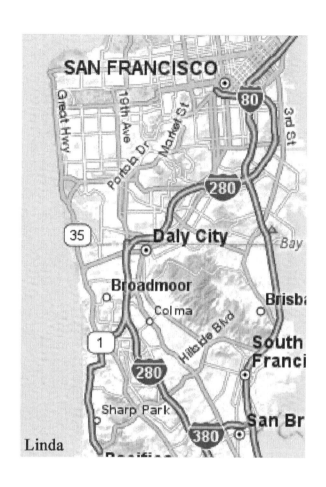

# Pacifica and San Francisco

I haven't lived in Pacifica for almost a quarter century, but the town still puts me on a high, particularly when the light is clear and hard and the ocean is the blue of a mountain lake and the waves run down the beach with dancing white crests. I drive through it often enough, and sometimes I stop to catch a couple of waves. However, it's rare I get on the ground and really touch my past.

It was one of those days, late fall, sky like a crystal globe. I decided to take a walk along the berm that sepa-

rates the beach from the golf course and **ends at Mori Point.** The golf course, one of the few that I enjoy looking at, wraps around **Laguna Salada**, a small lake surrounded by cypress trees, a kind of a natural area contrasting with the long stretches of unnaturally green grass. The beach was deserted, and the surf small and uninteresting.

Even though it was a weekday, people were out in droves, hiking, jogging, and walking their dogs. As I strolled down the berm, I looked at the great, tan protruding mass of hill that is Mori Point. It was pretty much as I'd left it in the late 80s, open, wild and free of man-made decorations, almost. I saw that there was a path that zig-zagged up hill to the top, where there seemed to be a bench. As an alternate to the path, there was what appeared to be a long stairway leading almost straight up the side of the hill to the bench.

I remembered when I used to hike there, over the ruts made by people on dirt bikes and off road vehicles, using the place unofficially, if not illegally. I could walk out there almost any day and rarely have company. Now, it is just part of the wonderful network of hiking paths along the Pacifica coast.

A few weeks later, in a rain storm, I walked it again, almost alone, and at the bottom of the stair way was a sign about Mori Point and how it was now part of the Golden Gate National Recreation Area, saved, protected, open to everyone, and never to be built upon. As I hiked to the top of the 184 steps and looked around, I felt so happy that the battle over this piece of coast was won by the advocates of public access.

In the 80s, as a member of Friends of Pacifica, I helped in the fight to preserve the place, to keep out a line of two story homes and a vast convention center that was proposed for the end of the point. There was also to be a four-lane freeway and other "improvements," but now the views take my breath away, just as they did the first time I came over the hill and saw the town rising out of the morning mist.

Pacifica is a chain of neighborhoods, separated by hills, and each neighborhood has its own personality. Vallemar is the most tucked away and invisible to the traveler, a narrow valley bordered by steep hills. I once went hiking with some folks in the hills in back of Vallemar, mostly on seldom-used local trails or simply bushwhacking. One of the men grew up there and said they had a group as teens. They called themselves Vallemar Liberation Front, but they weren't criminals or anything like that, just kids who liked to prank the neighborhood. They annoyed the adults, and the police were always chasing them, but they had these little hiding places in the brush, little forts, and the police couldn't get them. They finally got busted, and the VLF became history.

Even when I lived there, all I had to do was hike a couple

hundred yards behind almost any neighborhood and I'd find old sofas, tables, ice chests, folding chairs and sometimes beer cans. The local teens all had their get away places, and one was quite ornate and big enough to accommodate close to two dozen kids. It was a great place until some kid forgot to put out his cigarette and

 started a fire that almost spread to the neighborhood. The parents weren't crazy about having their houses burned down, so another kid hideout was lost.

**Linda Mar Beac**h is the main beach, and the parking lot is always full, any day of the week, any time of the year. The local surfers, who extend from tots to senior citizens, go out in any condition. I've seen hundreds sitting in two foot unsurfable slop. However, the next beach north, Rockaway, is a serious surfing place, with a channel to paddle out and often some powerful waves.

People used to drive into Rockaway, a run down place with a couple of good restaurants and some ancient second hand and hardware stores. There was a patch of dirt where surfers parked. Then a redevelopment agency was formed, the shabby buildings leveled, the long time shopkeepers chased out. Then nice, boring, new buildings were built, rented to trendy stores, and the dirt parking lot got pavement and a changing room, and something was gained, while something was lost. Progress always has two faces.

Three of the few places left from before redevelopment are Nick's Restaurant and the Sea Breeze Motel, both facing the beach. The food is good at Nick's, and the rooms are reasonable at the Sea Breeze. The Acapulco Mexican Food near Nick's is the other original business.

Mori Point is north of Rockaway, and there's a small cove beach there that had a rope tied to a metal stake, which was the only way down to the beach, one that wasn't used much. North of the point is the golf course and then another neighborhood, with a small shopping center. That's also the location of the town pier, and along that strand of beach they've made a nice promenade and a one way street with parking, so people can finally enjoy the beach without having to walk a couple of blocks, but hardly anyone used that beach. The pier, however, always has fishermen.

At the south end of that promenade, just before the golf course, there used to be the home of a man I knew. He said, "My place sat right there until the big storm of '83." I looked and said, "I don't see anything but a sliver of beach," and he said, "Exactly." Must have been one hell of a storm.

For the hiker, trails are everywhere. Every ridgeline that drops to Highway One has a trail running up it: across from Mori Point, across from Rockaway Beach, behind Oceana High School and out of San Pedro Valley County Park. They all converge at the top of the hill where Pacifica ends at an area that's mostly part of

So. from Montara Mtn

the Golden Gate National Recreation Area. The high school backs up to Milagra Ridge County Park, a big, grass-covered ridge with great views. One can hike all the way into the San Francisco Water Department land and on to **Montara Mountain**, the high point at eighteen hundred and some feet. And, just below the mountain is San Pedro County Park, where I was a docent for a time, and where some local man took time off work and built a trail from the existing park trails up to the mountain, allowing people to get to the top without trespassing on San Francisco's land. There is now an official trail, something over 3 miles each way from the visitor center in the park to the top of the mountain, a spot that gives a **360 degree view of the San Francisco Bay** area, and is well worth the hike.

To get to the park, take Linda Mar Blvd. at the signal, and go about three miles to the end. Make a right and a quick left into

the park.
The Shelldance
Bromeliad &
Orchid Nursery
is across from
Mori Point, and
it's an exit from
Highway One
only going
north. There's a
parking lot above the nursery, and from there you can hike up

**Sweeney Ridge**, where you can connect to the Portola Discovery Site, hike over into San Bruno or connect with the trail to

Montara Mountain. Another access to this trail system is by taking Fassler Avenue, the signal at Rockaway Beach, up the hill to where it meets Terra Nova Blvd. Also, you can hike up Mori Point from the golf course or from Rockaway Beach, the north parking lot.

San Pedro County Park's visitor center is informative and well designed and is worth taking a few minutes to explore. The trail up San Pedro Creek, which starts near the visitor center, is lovely and forested, dark and cool. There is also a ridge trail with nice views and a meadow to hike through, and the early riser might catch sight of one of the resident bobcats.

The creek flows out of the park and through town to the beach, and steelhead come up to spawn. Unfortunately, unsportsmanlike-like fishermen would sit by the stream and catch the helpless fish as they tried to spawn. It was illegal, but if no one was looking, they got away with it. We were looking. We'd take up positions along known spawning areas, set up a lawn chair, camera in hand. Anyone trying to take a fish would get a photo sent to Fish and Game, and that discouraged most of them. We actually started having some good runs of young fish until someone back flushed the high school swimming pool, chlorinating a big stretch of the creek and killing a generation of fingerlings.

Every year we also cleaned the creek, pulling out all kinds of human castoffs, like shopping carts, tires, even appliances. People seemed to think the creek was their private dump, and that attitude is why so many of the places we live are trashed and almost uninhabitable. Through community effort, the creek is still viable and uncluttered.

Living there, I'd often stop at the bottom of a ridge and just start walking. Before long, the beach and ocean were spread out below me, and the houses and businesses melted into the background. The only sounds were the wind and the birds, and I was out in nature while on a short walk from home.

Pacifica was a sleepy little town, and now it's a sleepy little town with some nice trails along the coastal bluffs. It was a good place to live, and I'd gladly live there again.

One of the battles in the '80s was over the proposal to bisect McNee Ranch State park with a huge freeway toward Half Moon Bay. This was tied in with the proposal to put the freeway all the way through town. It was about development interests south of Devil's Slide, and the Slide was unsuitable for a massive number of commuters. The freeway was defeated, and now a tunnel is nearing completion. It will avoid Devil's Slide, a place where granite formations meet sedimentary formations, with the unstable meeting sliding out periodically, during heavy rain years.

Devil's Slide is aptly named. It's cut into the side of a very unstable cliff. Driving along it, I used to marvel at the uplifted sedimentary rock formations, angled up at sixty to eighty degrees. Some very rapid and violent geological activity took place there recently, in geological time, that is. It was all sea bed, and then, pop, up it came, and now it wants to go back to the sea, and the road crews have had to fight with nature and gravity in this area for years. Soon, it will be left to crumble into the sea, and we'll lose the hassle along with the stunning views of Pedro Point.

The last neighborhood heading south is Shelter Cove,

which is bordered by Pedro Point, now reached via the Linda Mar Blvd. intersection, the last light before Devil's Slide. Pedro Point is a neighborhood that runs from the end of Linda Mar Beach up the steep hill, but there are a dozen or more houses actually down in the cove, which once was reachable by road, but the road has fallen away, leaving only a walking trail. Drive out San Pedro Avenue until it ends at Kent Road, and go left up to the top of the hill and park. You can look down into the cove, and maybe feel as I do, that

romantic notion about how delightful it would be to live there, tucked away from the rest of the world.

A treat awaits the person exploring this small area, Barolo's Restaurant serves up some excellent Italian food, and it's on San Pedro Rd. a couple of blocks west of Highway One.

The north end of Pacifica, the **Manor District** and beyond has a beach that's hard to reach. It's at the foot of a bluff, one that grows higher as you approach Daly City. This bluff is nothing more than a massive sand dune that's been sort of compressed into something that looks like solid ground. The slightest hint of rain belies that, and houses and apartments built along the bluffs have slipped or are slipping into the ocean. To get a real feel for the area, take Palmetto Avenue north, and take the left out to Mussel Rock. There's a parking area, and trails in the sand you can walk or slide down to reach the beach.

While living there, my wife and I decided one day to explore the remnants of the old road from San Francisco to Pacifica, the one built along the sandy bluffs, the new Skyline Drive is set back past several blocks of those little boxes, made of ticky tacky, made famous in the old pop song. We parked at Thornton Beach State Park in Daly City, a place that used to have beach access. We walked down what was left of the crumbling old road, which in

111

places was only a foot path. Then, near the highest part of the bluffs, the road ended. It stopped before a wide area where the sandy bluff had simply slumped. There was a bit of the road thirty or forty yards away, but nothing just ahead. We sat on the edge and slid over, sliding slowly down to the beach as if on snow. We walked the rest of the way to Pacifica, and as you may have guessed, we were all alone, save for one fisherman at Mussel Rock.

Before you leave Pacifica, make a quick stop at Florey's Book Co. on Palmetto Avenue in the Sharp Park area. It's off the freeway and near where the town pier is located, and the pier is a favorite of local fishermen. You can access Sharp Park from Paloma Ave or Clarendon Avenues. There are also a number of places to eat or have a drink on Palmetto. But, about Florey's; it's been a fixture in Pacifica for a long time. Florey, who owned it for many years, has died, but her grandson is keeping up the small book store tradition.

San Francisco has been written up extensively in every West Coast tour book, and there is little for me to add. I've worked there and lived there, but rarely have I been a tourist. I certainly couldn't begin to advise anyone on the better hotels or even restaurants. Most of the eateries I used to frequent have gone out of business or changed hands.

However, since you've just hiked up the hill from the beach at Thornton Beach Park, and you've done Pacifica, you must be headed into the city. So, my first question is do you like to hang glide or even watch others do it? If it's a yes to either, and the wind is blowing, which it does about 350 days a year, stop at Fort Funston Park. It's just north of Thornton and at the southern end of San Francisco. Turn left and drive to the parking lot near the bluffs. This is a popular place for people who love to jump off sand dunes with some aluminum and fabric strapped to their backs. They glide along, just overhead, and only the beginners crash into the surf, so don't expect exciting wipeouts.

The Great Highway runs along Ocean Beach, home of some pretty heavy surf, and most of the time you'll find some surfers out. If you'd rather stop at the zoo, it's at the beginning of Great Highway at Sloat Blvd. Look for the signs. **The zoo** has been

radically redone since I lived in the area. It's far more natural looking, with more modern enclosures, and it's now one of the better
zoos.

The Great Highway also runs
right by the end of Golden Gate Park,
and while I'm not going to describe the
park, there is the Beach Chalet Brewery
& Restaurant  at the foot of the park,
across from the beach. It's always
crowded, but the food and beer are
worth stopping for. The park also has a
wonderful art museum and a world
class natural history museum, the California Academy of Sciences,
complete with a walk through rain forest and a living roof.

Don't forget to walk around the ruins of Sutro Baths, just
past the **Cliff House**, as the road turns away from the water.

How-
ever, if
you are
a bicy-
clist,
there is
a won-
derful
coastal
ride.
Beside the Great Highway, at Sloat, there's a biking and walking
trail. It runs along the beach to the foot of Golden Gate Park,
which you cross to the beach side and continue north, then up the
hill to the Cliff House, where you might want to stop for lunch.
Continue up the wide sidewalk to the signal at the top of the hill,
above Sutro Baths and turn left. The road ends at a parking lot in a
couple blocks. This is Land's End, and there you can pick up the
Land's End Trail along the entrance to the Golden Gate and over to
Lincoln Park and down to the Sea Cliff neighborhood. A few
blocks further and you are headed up Lincoln Blvd. toward the
Golden Gate Bridge. The bridge has a hiking and biking path, and
on the Marin County side, you can take the first right down to

Sausalito. Go both ways, and you've spent a full day with views of the ocean and San Francisco Bay.

You've certainly read about Fisherman's Wharf, Pier 39, Chinatown and the boat ride out to Alcatraz, so I'll just alert you to special places that are not that famous. Actually, when you reach the end of Chinatown, at Broadway, you are right around the corner from two wonderful cultural must stops. One is City Lights Bookstore, 261 Columbus Avenue, owned by the poet Lawrence Ferlinghetti. It is the consummate bookstore, and it makes you feel oh so literary and intellectual just walking into the place. And if you don't find what you want there, almost diagonally at 540 Broadway, you'll find the **Beat Museum.** Take the $5 tour, even if the Beat Generation isn't your thing. It's an interesting part of recent history. And while you're there, have a chat with Jerry, the owner. Tell him Meade sent you.

This is Jerry's labor of love. He started it in Monterey and moved it to the City, in part because that was where the beat thing was happening in the 1950s. Jerry has a small but really interesting selection of books there, so don't leave empty handed.

You've seen all the tourist stops, and hopefully, you've also taken my suggestions. There's only one thing to do before leaving the City and officially entering Northern California: Walk across the Golden Gate Bridge. Yes, park on either side, grab your camera and a wind breaker—it's windy 364 days a year on the bridge— and walk over and back. If it's not socked in with fog, you'll get some stunning views of the city along with some exercise on a good one hour walk. At the other end of the bridge, you've entered Marin County.

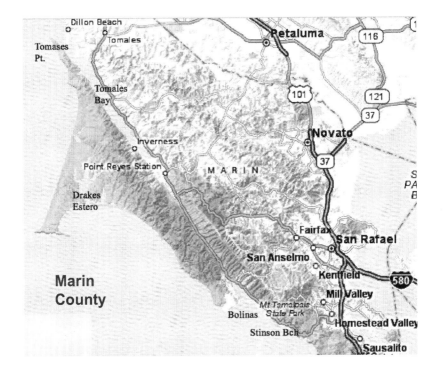

## Marin County

Marin County is probably one of the most desirable places in the world to live. Most of the towns, small and picture perfect, shout the comfortable, affluent lifestyle. It's a county of boats, bike trails, boutiques and B & Bs. Add to that the ease of spending a day in San Francisco, without having to live with the noise and congestion, and what's not to love about it? Well, for one thing, the cost of buying there isn't terribly lovable unless you have bags of money.

It may cost a lot to live there, but, if you are self contained, you can camp—unofficially—high up on the ridge, south of Stinson Beach for free, along a long dirt pullout.

First, you have to go over the bridge and not stop at the usually packed **parking and scenic view spot** on the Marin side. There are better places to look back at the city. Take the first exit, which gives you two options. You can go to the right, down into Sausalito to wander around the cute shops and eat at any of a dozen great little restaurants or have a drink almost anywhere. That's being a tourist, and if you are in that mood, look for the Lisa Kristine photo gallery. I have a lot of photo artist friends, and it's all nice work, but this woman is to color photos what Ansel Adams was to black and white.

But, you are reading this because you love the coast, its scenery, the sense of exploration. In that case, after you exit, go left either through the tunnel on Bunker Road, and out toward Point Bonita, or take the high road up the hill, over the "Golden Gate," with amazing views. That road drops down later and joins Bunker. However you go, you'll end up at Point Bonita, where there's a lighthouse. Off the point is a place called the Potato Patch, where a freighter filled with potatoes went down many years ago, causing a shallow spot where huge waves break on big winter swells. Ever see a seventy-foot wave?

Out past the point is old Fort Cronkhite, which has a visitor center. There is also the Marine Mammal Center, a place where they rescue seals, sea lions and otters. You can visit, and since you'll be touched by the care given to these hapless creatures, you'll be sure to put a few bucks in the donation box when you leAvenue However, talk to the staff and volunteers. They are caring and interesting people.

There's a super hollow surf break near the visitor center, and there are miles of trails running along the bluffs and down Tennessee Valley. This is all part of the Golden Gate National Recreation Area, and you could walk all the way to Muir Beach, where Highway One reconnects with the coast. The GGNRA has very well marked trails, good signage and distances marked off, so you won't get in too deep or get lost.

You can't drive from the point to Muir Beach. You must go back to 101 and continue north to the Highway One exit. As you turn on Highway One, you'll see that there are some waterways extending inland under the highway bridge. There's some park-like areas and bike trails, just north of Highway One, and you can pull over. If you have a bike, there are miles of the best of Marin at your fingertips. If you have a kayak, just start paddling out, under the highway, past Sausalito, into Richardson Bay, past the multi, multi-million homes at Belvedere and Tiburon and through Raccoon Strait to Angel Island, about six miles each way. If you're not the adventure type, you can take Blithedale Avenue, a bit further up 101 and go out to the ferry in Tiburon. Either way, Angel Island is a lovely place, miles of hiking trails, beaches and awesome views of the city and the rest of the Bay Area. Still, in my opinion, it's a bit better if you paddle the hour or so to get there, leaving your kayak in some deserted cove and walking around.

My mistake when I first kayaked the area was not to notice the parking area west of the highway. Rather, being a weekend, the business park right off 101 was empty, so I parked there and slipped my kayak into the water. It was a great paddle out to the point, and then the channel was a bit rough, but it's a narrow channel, so not a problem. After pulling up on an Angle Island beach and walking to the main beach where the ferry boat lands and there is food and drink, I paddled back into a strong wind, which was a bit of a pain, but not the bad part. That was when I landed and real-

ized that the tide had dropped while I was gone, and there was now twenty feet of deep, gooey mud between me and the parking lot. And, yes, the mud never, ever washes out of your clothes.

Better to launch at a dog park in Mill Valley: Highway One exit; when One turns left, go straight on Miller to Camino Alto. Turn right and right again on Sycamore Avenue and park in the lot at the end of the road. Paddle under the Highway One bridge, and if not interested in Angel Island, stay to the right and explore the floating city of **Sausalito's houseboats**, which come in all shapes and sizes.

But, let's go back to the Highway One exit and assume you are anxious to get back to where the sea is beside you. Highway One takes you by Muir Woods National Monument, which on a summer weekend always has parking lot full signs along the route. If that's when you are in the area, don't worry. There's a place just as nice a few miles further, in the next county. Like Muir Woods in Marin, Armstrong Redwoods near the Russian River is also a beautiful redwood park, Muir is national, and Armstrong is state.

Muir Beach is a lovely place to stop, a quiet, scenic little cove. Muir Beach Overlook, a bit further up the hill, is good for a quick stop for the view. Any sign about an overlook, is worth a stop. Someone thought it was worth a sign and some parking spots.

Past the overlook the road runs along the ridge — where I've pulled over for the night at a long dirt shoulder at the top of the ridge— before winding, and I mean winding, down to Stinson Beach. On that stretch, and you have to watch for the sign, you'll find Slide Ranch. They have parking, and it's open for picnics and hiking through their pastures and along this dramatic coast. You can also reserve accommodations.

There's free parking at Stinson, restrooms and places to eat in walking distance from the beach. The beach is wide and inviting, and sometimes it isn't foggy, and sometimes the surf is even good. There's also a pretty good coffee kiosk along the highway, at the stop sign at Calle Del Mar. If you turn up that hill, make a right at the next intersection, a left on Laurel, another left on Belvedere and a right on Avenida Farralone, you find a trailhead at the top of the road. This has given you a good head start on a hike to the top of the ridge at Mt. Tamalpais State Park. There's a road up there, West Ridgecrest Blvd., which you can also access from Bolinas Rd, five miles further north. However, if you miss this trail head, there are several others scattered along the next 7 or 8 miles, each one affording unrestricted coastal views.

Once you pass Stinson Beach, you'll follow Bolinas Lagoon for four or five miles. You'll notice a couple of places to pull over on the water side, places with a small sign. These are good spots to bird watch, fish or launch a kayak, something I highly recommend.

Audubon Canyon Ranch is across from Bolinas Lagoon. They have some nice hiking trails and guided walks, and, as you might imagine, you'll see some birds on your hike.

Any trip, even a brief one, to **Bolinas,** on the ocean side of

the lagoon, is an escape from the rush hour, fast food rat race of contemporary California life and all that's become routine in our cities. If you can fit in a couple hours of paddling, you've had a perfect get away. However, before you decide to kayak, make sure you check the tides.

On a very high tide you can paddle pretty much anywhere in **Bolinas Lagoon** without concern. At low tides there are mud

flats that can get the un-wary paddler stuck in something resembling black glue. I learned that the hard way on my first trip, where I had to drag my kayak through 60 feet of mud, losing a sport sandal in the process.

It you launch along the highway, by one of those signs, going south is mostly clear paddling. Just remember that the deeper parts of this shallow lagoon are along the edges, so approach the middle with a wary eye.

As the lagoon narrows to the south, it becomes channels that lead almost into Stinson Beach. This is a great area for up close bird watching, with egrets standing along the banks, and the paddle along the ocean side takes you past some lovely beachfront homes.

You can also paddle in from the mouth, at the end of Wharf Road, in Bolinas. From there you can either turn right toward Stinson or continue east toward Highway One. Doing so will take you along side a large mud flat usually lined with seals, gulls and pelicans. This mud flat recedes as the tide goes up, but part of it is an island that is always above water. However, just inside the entrance channel, you can turn left and paddle the deep channel along side the town, with boats tied up behind houses, giving you an alternate view of this quaint town.

Shortly, the houses give way to a wooded area which eventually opens up to typical wetlands vegetation. Ideally, on a high tide, you can paddle almost to the northern end of the lagoon and return along Highway One in a long loop. This, however, is where I got in trouble on my first visit.

The tide was dropping as I passed the houses, the wooded area and into the northern branch of the lagoon. Then, as I could see it getting shallower, I turned toward the highway. I could see obvious deep water just ahead, but there was a patch that looked dicey. I thought, having a shallow draft, I could pick my way through this short section. I was wrong. You'd be surprised how long it takes to pull a kayak through 60 feet of knee-deep mud.

There is one other thing that can make a fun day unpleasant. Sometimes a stiff wind comes up in the afternoon, as it did on my most recent trip. The day was sunny and calm when I led my friends into the channels for some bird watching, but as we headed back, a howling wind suddenly came up, and the relaxed chatting gave way to some serious paddling against a rising chop.

On a day when the ocean swells are small and few surfers are out, an option is to also paddle out and play in the long rolling waves that break just out from the mouth, and if the ocean is very calm, you can paddle a couple miles north to Duxbury Reef, which shelters the beaches of Bolinas. I did this once at low tide and was able to explore the extensive tide pools close up.

As you drive by the lagoon, you'll pass Audubon Canyon Ranch, which may or may not be open. Then, at the northern end of the lagoon, the first left will lead you to the town of Bolinas. There are no signs directing you to the town, as the locals cut them down as fast as the state puts them up. Needless to say, it's a quirky little village. You'll make a left, a left and another left at the nursery, pass the school and arrive in Bolinas at the junction of the two streets, Brighton and Wharf, both of which will take you to the most charming beach you'll ever walk.

Actually, at high tide there's not much beach at all, but a low tide, you can walk all the way north to Duxbury Reef, a series of rock stepping stones that extend close to a mile off shore and which keep the waters of town fairly calm when the rest of the coast is churning whitecaps. It's about an hour round trip and one of my favorite beach walks.

To explore the tide pools and beaches north of the point, go back through town to Mesa Road, turn right to Overlook Drive, and turn left to Elm, where you'll turn right and go out to the end of the road. There is a park-ing lot where you can walk down to the beach or up the hill to the bluff overlooking the point. Be careful up there, as the cliffs are unsta-ble, and it's straight down to the rocks.

If you're an **art lover, you'll enjoy the walls** along the beach, all painted with the most stun-ning, creative graffiti. This is way better than the bor-ing stuff you see on city factory walls. Bolinas is a rather creative town in a very offbeat kind of way.

There are a couple of nice places to eat in Bolinas, on Wharf Road, along with Smiley's, a really fun little bar in a very old building. And they often have live music on weekends. If you've never stopped for a cold one at Smiley's, you're not a North Coast traveler.

Once you've wandered the beach, caught some of the surf that draws people from miles around and checked out the town, there's one more side trip for the traveler who's not in a big hurry. Go back to the stop sign just after you exit town, Mesa Rd. Turn left, and about three miles out, you'll see the Point Reyes Bird Ob-servatory. Then the pavement ends, but the road is still good, and another mile will take you to the end and the Palomarin Trailhead, a jumping off spot for some good hikes in the Golden Gate

National Recreation Area. There are several little lakes and some nice wild stretches of coast reachable from this trailhead. There's

even **a waterfall** at the beach some four miles in, but the climb down to the bottom of the falls is treacherous.

Once back on Highway One, between Bolinas and Point Reyes Station, there are a number of other trails going east up the ridge or west toward the coast. Two trail hubs are at Five Brooks and at the Bear Valley Visitor center near Olema. The visitor center and park headquarters has a very large parking lot, information and one of the most popular trails in the park. The Bear Valley trail, fire road most of the way, is four miles to the coast and a scenic viewpoint. The trail, mostly through lovely woods, rises slowly before descending again to the coast. If you'd rather ride, it is accessible by bicycle until the last half mile, and there are places to lock up the bike.

Olema has a both a Deli and a fairly pricey restaurant. Just north of town is a private campground, Olema RV Resort and Campground, right on the highway. 415.663.8106 or ed@olemarvresort.com. It's $30 plus a night to camp there, but Samuel P. Taylor State Park, in a redwood forest, five miles inland from Olema, is about the same price.

**Olema Valley**

Besides being adjacent to wetlands, and a short drive to Point Reyes, this campground is also just a few minutes from the Station House Cafe in Point Reyes Station, less than two miles away, one of my favorite eating and drinking establishments in West Marin.

At Olema, you can take Bear Valley Road to Limantour Road and a winding eight to ten mile drive to Limantour Beach, another great beach with an extensive network of hiking trails along the bluffs and above and around fingers of Drakes Estero. You can also pick up Limantour Road a couple miles north, just before Point Reyes Station. Turn left on Sir Francis Drake to Inverness Park, and take Drakes Summit Road to Limantour Road.

Point Reyes Station is a major junction, as just south of town there is the junction to Point Reyes, itself, Sir Francis Drake Blvd., a huge recreation area. But the town is more than a junction. Besides a great place to eat lunch and dinner, there's an excellent bakery in the middle of town, along with the Pine Cone Diner, a local's favorite for breakfast, on 4th Street. There are excellent art galleries in town, including Christine DeCamp's gallery on 4th, right where the highway turns to the right. Drop in and see Christine's interesting and unusual art, and tell her I sent you.

Sir Francis Drake is a left, just south of Point Reyes Station. It takes you out to Point Reyes Peninsula and Point Reyes National Seashore. This piece of the Pacific Tectonic Plate, which is slowly disengaging itself from most of North America, could be and probably is material enough for a full book. Check into the campground in Olema, and spend a couple of days exploring.

Once you've turned left on Sir Frances Drake Blvd. and driven over the strip of wetland that connects the peninsula to the rest of the country, you'll enter the one town on the peninsula, Inverness. As you drive through town, you'll see Blue Water Kayaking (http://www.bwkayak.com/), where you can take a tour or rent a kayak and explore. They are located at the inner end of Tomales Bay, near where the bay becomes winding channels. On the left, there's a pizza and beer place, or if you like something a bit fancier, Vladimir's Czechoslovakian Restaurant is probably the only high end eatery on the peninsula.

After you leave Inverness and turn away from the bay, the

road splits, with Pierce Point Rd. going off to the right and Sir Francis Drake continuing on to the left. On Sir Francis Drake, there are three roads going off to the left. The first is Mt. Vision Overlook, where you can drive up and look over the point and the estero. The next leads to the parking area for the Estero Trailhead, for those who want to hike around the east side of Drake's Estero and almost out to the beach. The third leads to the **Oyster Farm**, where you can buy oysters or launch a kayak.

**Drakes Estero is a four fingered bay**, and you can paddle into the various fin-

gers, paddle around the oyster beds, watch the bat rays that seem to be flying through the water and end up out near the beach. It's a beautiful place to paddle, and once you leave the oyster farm, it seems like you've left the civilized world.

A bit further on the road and you are between the estero and the beach. There are three roads to the right to beaches where you can walk and play, but remember that the open waters of the peninsula are dangerous, so if you're not a strong swimmer or surfer, stay on the beach.

A left takes you to Drakes Beach in Drakes Bay, sheltered by the point and very calm most of the time. There's a ranger station there and a visitor center and miles of beach to walk. However Sir Francis Drake continues to the point and the lighthouse, located on the edge of the bluff at one of the foggiest places on the coast. You can walk out to the visitor center and then down 300 steps to the light itself. But remember, it's 300 steps back up again.

Heading back, turn left at the junction to Pierce Point, which is an adventure in itself. The first stop is Heart's Desire Beach, on the Tomales Bay side, a popular day use beach on the less foggy side. Further out the road as you start to glimpse the Pacific, there's a parking area for the hike to Abbotts Lagoon and the beach beyond. It's an interesting and scenic walk, with colorful coastal plants scattered among the dunes and lots of birds. The next beach, accessible by trail is Kehoe Beach. Then the road ends at Pierce Ranch, a well preserved ranch site, worth walking around and checking out. There are signs telling the visitors what was once there.

There's also another beach, McClures, a short walk from the parking area. However the real treat is the five mile hike out to the point. This trail goes up and down some, but there are no serious hills to climb. It's an unforgettable hike any time of year, but during the foggy summer, it is almost surreal.

Summer is fog season and the warm land sucks it in with awesome force. The result out on these unprotected coastal bluffs is fog that blows onshore so hard that one has to lean into it at times. The trail starts out behind the historical old ranch. I stepped off, and within a minute the ranch had vanished in the blowing fog.

In a way this is more than a hike, it's an excursion into the

very nature of the human thinking process. Since we have a left and a right side to our brains, we tend to mentally cut things in two: right and wrong, black and white, poor and rich, civilized and wild. **Tomales Point** acts as a symbol of that human tendency, with the wild, steep and foggy west side, and the calm, sunny, gentle bay side. The land narrows down until finally coming to a point, a point which juts north right at the margin of two huge tectonic plates. Tomales Point and the huge crustal plate it rides on plows its way north at two inches a year, leading a strip of land that includes Los Angeles and Baja California.

Along the entire walk, one is confronted with opposites. On the bay side, those gentle hills slope down to inlet coves and absolutely still beaches, and the trails wander down into the valleys, often with views of the herds of Elk that roam the area. On the ocean side the land crumbles away, creating rugged cliffs that hang out in space before plunging to pocket beaches constantly ravaged by restless surf. The inland side is done in brown and tan, while the ocean bluffs are decorated in brightly colored lichen. The fog comes off the ocean in giant waves, sometimes so thick that you can't see thirty feet in any direction. But at times it will suddenly clear, giving a momentary panorama that has the effect of a photo, a stroboscopic scene flash frozen in your mind for life. The scenery becomes abstract in the swirling fog, but you can find faint lines like the light pencil traces that can be found below the color in watercolor paintings. Then, just as you think the hint of some natural shape is playing hide and seek with you, the fog lifts for a moment, and a beautiful piece of coast, complete with beaches, waves, rocks, sea birds and offshore islands, stands brilliantly illuminated in the sun. Then you blink or look away, and it's gone, only to be replaced a moment later by another scene on the bay side.

Walking along, I caught occasional bright flashes of the scenery, exploding out of the fog, only to be engulfed again. With only one stand of trees, the wildlife has nothing to hide behind except the fog, so when you see them, it is a fleeting look at a nervous being. I saw something dark, waving off to the side, and it didn't look like a plant, so I got closer, only to find, as the fog cleared, a large skunk, shaking its tail and wondering why I wasn't getting the message. Then I realized that with the wind to my back, I'd have to be almost on top of the skunk to get sprayed. I watched for a moment before feeling sorry for it and stepping back on the trail.

The scenery is seductive, pulling you further and further in. There is one deep canyon leading way down to a deserted beach on the ocean side, a great eroded canyon that spirals down until the caves in the canyon wall are above you, the only shelter big enough for the local mountain lions and coyotes. At first the trail seems much too steep to climb down into, but you can walk a few yards to the edge for a better view. Those few yards reveal more trail, not too steep, to follow down to the next edge until you find yourself at the bottom, the ground wet from the tiny streamlet that trickles down from the canyon's head, the beach almost always deserted.

All along the trail out to Tomales Point, there are those amazing opposites, the soft contours and colors of the bay side, and the rugged and colorful ocean side. It's like a fractal. The complexity, instead of decreasing or staying the same as you get closer, increases. The total is a deep, intricate, wondrous maze. After passing the low point, with the trees and some standing water, the trail becomes indistinct as it wanders through the dunes toward the point. Standing up on the sandy bluffs brings it all together. You can see both sides from there, the calm bay and the angry ocean. You can look north to Bodega Head, emerging faintly from the gray. It's then that you feel like you're on a massive ship steaming slowly north.

By the time I got near the point I was obsessed. I had to know what was there. Was there a place that was neither ocean nor bay? A few yard's walk left me on a rise, maybe fifteen feet above the water. Here the trail split, dropping almost straight down to the bay and also to the ocean, the two opposites unresolved to the bitter end. And straight ahead was a half-submerged slab of rock, waves washing over it, crammed with a colony of sea birds, the point of contact between two unimaginably huge tectonic plates, the point where rocks are subducted and ground to molten pulp, one of the most wind-blown and storm-tossed places on the coast, and to these feathered creatures it was home.

It was more an experience than just a hike, and each time since then it has been almost a different place, changing moods with every slight change in the weather.

Across Tomales Bay Highway One continues north past Point Reyes Station, with lots of places to pullout and trail heads along the bay, and on to Marshall. There's another **Blue Water Kayaking in Marshall**, where you can rent or tour the bay. There are also a couple places to stop, Nick's Cove and Cottages, 23240 Shoreline Hwy and Tony's Seafood Restaurant at 18863 Shoreline

Hwy. At the north end of town, if you can really call Marshall a town, is the public boat ramp and parking lot. For a fee you can park and launch, directly across from **Hog Island**. Paddling or power boat-

ing over to Hog Island and on to one of the small coves on the point is a great little jaunt, unless the wind comes up, as it tends to do. Also from one of those coves it's pretty easy to hike up on the bluffs, past the grazing elk and on to the trail out to the point.

There's another place to launch about a mile further, after the highway turns away from the bay. On the left there's a sign for Keys Creek Fishing Access. There's a small parking lot just off the highway, a portable potty and a short walk to the tidal creek. From there, it takes perhaps a half hour to be out on the bay and another half hour to Hog Island. It's also possible to paddle in-land, and in about ten minutes **Keys Creek** continues into some narrow channels, and Walker Creek, the main channel goes under the highway and soon passes two ranch houses before winding into a thickly wooded narrow canyon. Eventually the creek becomes too choked with vegetation to continue, but for a short time a kayaker is taken back 100 years to a forgotten frontier California.

While the parking lot is not a campground, there are no signs prohibiting it, and there is a restroom of sorts, so I've spent the night there on several occasions. After about ten at night, the highway traffic dies down and the place is peaceful.

Away from the creeks, West Marin rolls gently along. Driving the highway feels like piloting a boat over gentle swells. It's beautifully rural. At the bottom of one long, gentle hill is another tiny West Marin town, Tomales. There's a great little bakery in the center of the two block long town, and the cross street leads out to Dillon Beach, some four miles away.

You can't park for free in Dillon Beach. There's parking lot at the beach that charges by the day, and there's an RV park. You can park temporarily at the little convenience store, but the rest of the town is restricted to residents. The beach sits at the mouth of Tomales Bay, directly across from the point. Long, slow waves wrap around the point and roll in, and there are often surfers in the water, despite the rumors of great white sharks.

When you take the road out of Dillon Beach, there's a junction. The right takes you back to Tomales, and the left to Valley Ford, which is on Highway One, just over the line in Sonoma County. However, just a mile before reaching Valley Ford, there's a little known, but outstanding  paddling experience, **Estero Americano**. The Valley Ford Franklin School Road crosses the Estero at Marsh Road, and just off the road there is a small parking area, just feet from the water. When you launch, go left.

130

One thing that makes the Estero special is that on hot summer days everyone flocks to the coast to escape the city and the heat. Unfortunately, you'll find most of the city is there, crowding the beaches and the parking. Imagine relaxing on a totally deserted beach at the mouth of Estero Americano, halfway between Dillon Beach and Bodega Bay.

There's a catch, however. You can't drive to it, and you probably can't even walk to it, unless perhaps at a very low tide. The only way in is to paddle for an hour and a half to two hours. Yet getting there is often at least as wondrous as being there.

That's the case with Estero Americano. The six mile paddle down the estero transports you to a California gone for 200 years, a sparsely populated rolling land of green and gold, cattle grazing on the hills.

Just after passing under the bridge there is a stretch of water populated with thousands of pale blue dragonflies. They dance in the air like fairies or like heat shimmers on a desert highway. With a little imagination they become a welcoming committee to a land of solitude.

Soon the Estero widens, birds pick for food along the marsh grasses, cows graze lazily on the hills and the occasional ranch house can be seen atop a distant hill.

After about an hour there is a channel going off to the left at a 90-degree angle. It flows to a bluff, turns and appears to intersect the main channel a quarter mile down stream. This is the one deceiving place on the trip. The left fork is the main channel, as I discovered when I had to walk my kayak through the mud and climb over a barbed wire fence.

This left channel takes the paddler by Whale-Tail Rock, a very distinctive formation. From this rock to the next rock formation, the water is very shallow, so one must take care not to go aground.

The Estero enters a steep-sided valley populated with egrets, herons, pelicans and gulls. As the canyon walls drop away, the beach appears a short way ahead.

In summer the Estero doesn't flow to the sea. In winter, when it does, it would be wise to take a tide table along, as low tide can be a muddy problem.

131

A ranch house way up on the hill reminds the paddler that he isn't totally alone, as the beach gives the impression of being visited for the very first time. Approaching the beautiful rock formations on the south end of the beach causes the nesting birds to take up an angry cry against the invading aliens.

These rock formations, surrounding crystal clear tide pools, give way to another, smaller beach, more sea rocks, and on and on, perhaps all the way to Dillon Beach. I walked through a sea arch and into the water to see yet another beach and point. It looked possible to walk to Dillon Beach on a minus tide, but I've yet to try it.

I wandered those beaches alone for an hour or more. This was on a hot, sunny Saturday in mid June. I didn't see other people until halfway back to the car.

Approaching the shallows at Whale-Tail Rock, I watched two kayaks growing closer. In a brief conversation with the couple, I discovered that they were among a small group of regular paddlers on this slough. A half hour later I passed a couple in a canoe, desperately maneuvering to keep from going aground.

Returning through a blue haze of dragonflies to my car, it seemed odd to find the tiny parking area filled with three vehicles. I had been out of touch for five glorious hours, and it took a few minutes to readjust to civilization.

Back on the road again in Sonoma County, it's just a short drive to Bodega Bay, a wonderful place to stop for lunch and exploration, but that's the next chapter.

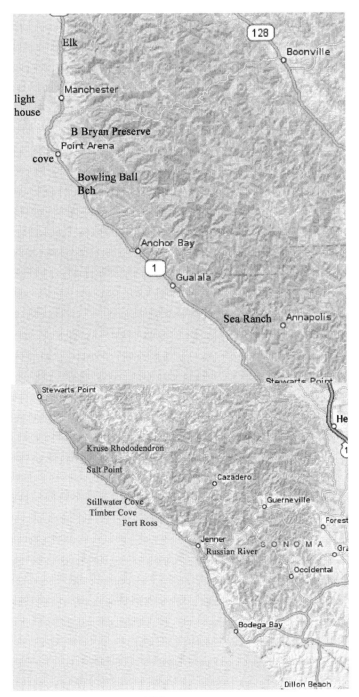

Elk

128

Boonville

Manchester

light
house

B Bryan Preserve

Point Arena

cove

Bowling Ball
Bch

Anchor Bay

1

Gualala

Sea Ranch    Annapolis

Stewarts Point

Stewarts Point

He

1

Kruse Rhododendron

Salt Point

Cazadero

Stillwater Cove

Guerneville

Timber Cove

Forest

Fort Ross

Jenner        S O N O M A    Gra

Russian River

Occidental

Bodega Bay

Dillon Beach

133

# Sonoma Coast (and Mendonoma)

Almost everyone has seen the Hitchcock classic, The Birds, set in Bodega Bay. **The Tides** restaurant where people gathered and cowered under the onslaught of the birds is still one of the most popular places in Bodega, a town with several good restaurants and places to stay. Greatly expanded

since the early 60's film, The Tides wharf, restaurant, bar, gift shop, market and lodging offers bay view dining, full bar, seafood market and a place to stay in the heart of the local action: 835 Coast Highway One, Bodega Bay. Restaurant: (707) 875-3652; Fish Market 707.875.3554; Gift Shop 707.875.3755; Gas Station & Mini Mart 707.875.9868.

Bodega Bay is a great place for boaters, and even kayakers can enjoy the bay, or Bodega Bay Harbor. A trip out to Bodega Head, via Bay Flat Rd. leads to a part of Sonoma Coast State Beach, with great hiking trails along the bluffs, where you can look down and marvel at the awesome power of the Pacific. Unfortunately, Bodega Head, Bodega Dunes and other Sonoma State Beach are either listed as closed or open seasonally. However, even when the gate is locked, you can usually park outside and walk in. To check on the parks: http://www.parks.ca.gov/?page_id=451

Bodega Bay is the closest thing to a city along the Sonoma Coast, and it has everything for the visitor, including eateries ranging from little fishermen's cafes to fancy dining, and lodging, including an RV park. It's a great town for the active outdoor visitor with fishing, whale watching, kayaking (rentals and tours) at Bodega Bay Kayak: (707) 875-8899. You can also rent surfboards at Bodega Bay Surf Shack (707) 875-3944, right in the heart of town, just off Highway One. However, the main surfing spot is Salmon Creek, just north of town, and it can be rather brutal.

There is also horseback riding on the beach at Chanslor Stables 2660 Coast Highway One, Bodega Bay (707) 875-2721. Bodega Bay Pro Dive offers a full service dive center: air fills, scuba lessons and equipment, 1275 Hwy 1, Bodega Bay (707) 875-3054.

So, even if you don't have your own ocean sports equipment, you can easily spend a long weekend at Bodega Bay, enjoying the unique ambiance. Also, if you bring your bike, the ride out to the end of Bodega Head is scenic and there isn't the traffic that infects the highway.

For traveling surfers, just north of town at Salmon Creek, there is parking along the bluff overlooking a long, lovely beach. Standing by the restrooms and looking at the ocean, you'll see, on

any decent surf day, a crowd in the water. This is a premier surf spot, and unless it's quite small, it breaks with a vengeance. In other words, beginners take a long look before entering the water. There's also a state park campground at Salmon Creek.

Between Salmon Creek and the Russian River is about eight miles, and most of the coast between the two is part of the **Sonoma Coast State**

**Beaches.** The good news about this is that there are parking areas and trails down to the beach, all open to the public, all along the way. The bad news is

that they have signs up that say no camping, so you probably would be chased off if you pulled over for the night. However it's a lovely stretch of beach, Duncan's Landing being one of my favorites.

Just before going down the hill to cross the Russian River,

135

there's a left turn for **Goat Rock,** part of the Sonoma County State Beaches. As you drive into the park, there are trailheads along the left, including some parking areas, and I've found some of these closed off recently. One of these affords a

trail all the way down to the beach. On the right side of the road is a fence at the private property line. You can see when you pull off to park that there is a mile or two of beaches and coves, rock formations jutting out into the surf and scenic bluffs above them.

Continuing down the hill, the road splits. To the right is a big parking area at the long sand spit that separates the Russian River estuary from the ocean. You can walk down the beach to the mouth of the river and the colony of seals that often haul out there. If the seals are there, remember they are protected, so don't do anything to flush them. Let them rest and walk back.

I remember an early June day, when there was no wind and almost no people, and nothing was moving. I walked down the beach, passing a vulture sitting on a log on the beach. It was a total still-life scene, except for the vulture's bright eyes, which followed me as I moved. It felt, just for a moment, as if time had stopped, and that's the impression I get at Goat Rock, a place somehow out of time, with the endless pounding of the surf and the glassy waters of the river mouth.

Rather than turn right to the big parking area, turning left leads to a one-lane road and to another parking area by the big rock. Next to that rock is a beach that is often surfed, but seldom worth surfing. If the tide is low, you can walk a mile or more down the beach, finding a cove where you can experience solitude.

One thing to note is that on the right (north) side of the big rock, the beach drops away steeply into the surf line, and the waves break almost on the beach, causing a tumbling action that's almost

136

impossible to escape. This is a very dangerous place, so don't go in the water.

As you walk the long strand and look over the mouth of the river, the town of Jenner sits on the other side, a quarter mile swim or a two mile drive. Jenner, at the mouth of the Russian River, is the jumping off point for the North Coast. It's a picturesque village set on the hill above the river. Accommodations are limited to the Jenner Inn, a bed and breakfast, and the River's End, charming cottages and a restaurant on a bluff overlooking the mouth of the river.

Heading down the road north of Goat Rock, just before crossing the river and entering Jenner, there's a great, and very inexpensive place to eat. The Sizzling Tandoor is at 9960 Highway 1, (707) 865-0625. You like Indian food, but you don't like paying high prices? Stop there, as there isn't much else in Jenner except

at River's End Inn, (707) 865-2484, www.ilovesunsets.com.

**River's End** is a great place to stay, perched on the bluff over the mouth of the river and facing the sunset. The night I stayed there, in November, when the Inn is barely open, there had been a storm, and the late afternoon sky was lined with clouds. I sat on the deck and watched one of the most colorful sunsets I can recall. Note the name of their website. Also, the lovely, rustic cabins have comfortable beds and no TV, which means sitting on the deck with a glass of wine until the sun sets and then settling into the plush bed with a good book. I don't think I've ever awakened as refreshed as I did that morning. River's End does have a full bar and restaurant, more expensive than The Sizzling Tandoor, but more upscale and with a more varied menu. Their special dish is North American elk for $43 (subject to change).

There's also a bed and breakfast, Jenner Inn & Cottages, in

137

town, but I've never stayed there, so I can't say much about it, other than you don't get the sunsets.

If you have your own boat or kayak, there's a launch ramp right in town. You can't miss it as you drive Highway One through town and past a little gift store on the left. On a calm summer day with minimal tidal changes, you can paddle out through the mouth, through the surf and explore all the little rock islands that dot that piece of coast. However, most people explore the wide  mouth and the island in the middle, before **paddling upstream** through marshland mazes on the south side or up the main channel toward Duncans Mills. Also, across from the dock there's a van, trailer and stack of kayaks. These belong to WaterTreks (www.watertreks.com), and they have rentals and and an interesting assortment of eco tours. Even if you don't usually kayak, this place is a treat.

Before you continue north into the sparsely populated "Mendonoma" coast, turn inland on the 116 and go about four miles to **Duncans Mills**. While it looks like a wide spot along the  road, it has a rich history that you can sample at the railroad station turned museum. There are also art galleries, kayak rentals on the Russian River, antique stores, gift shops and one of the best restaurants in the area. Small and intimate, the Cape Fear Café serves breakfast, lunch and dinner, and the prices are reasonable to moderate. The menu is varied, with a good selection of wine and beer, and there is something for even the most sophisticated taste. Since opening in 1997, it's been a popular stop, even in the off season. I always stop when in the area. It's right off the highway on the north side, along with the other cute shops and art galleries in old-fashion buildings.

On the south side of 116, if you just want a quick snack and coffee, the Gold Coast Coffee & Bakery is a place I like to visit just before or after a kayak trip on the lower Russian River. And, it's a great place to kayak, so if you have the time, contact Renee (Angel) Garcia or Peter L. Nardone 25375 Steelhead Blvd. PO Box 99 Duncans Mills, CA 95430.

You can continue up river for a few minutes to the little river town of Guerneville, home of several cafes and a charming bookstore. It's also where you turn to Armstrong Redwoods State Reserve. If you missed your walk in the redwoods way back at Muir Woods, here's another chance. Park in the lot outside the park entrance and walk in without having to pay. You can camp there also, and if interested, ask the ranger. It's a great place for an hour or two hiking among the big trees, along a small stream. You can also bike to the park from Guerneville, which takes about 20 minutes. In fact, biking along the Russian River on 116 is a delight, almost flat and a better way to see the sights.

## Mendonoma Coast

A few yards beyond River's End a section of coast known as the Mendonoma Coast begins. This 80-mile, sparsely inhabited stretch of winding asphalt is strung with occasional beads of settlements with populations in the dozens or hundreds. As the name implies, this is part Sonoma and part Mendocino Counties.

North of Jenner the hills jut straight up from the sea, and Highway One twists from one scenic view to the next. There are a few places to stop and wander around. Among those is Russian Gulch Beach, part of Sonoma Coast State Park. At my last visit the parking area was closed, another victim of the budget, so look for a wide shoulder, park and walk back. From the parking lot, you take a short walk through a dappled, deciduous forest, along a small creek, to a cove beach with small waves lapping the sand and a gravel beach. Vista Trail is another part of the park with the parking closed off. It's a couple miles north and several hundred feet higher. The mile loop includes an impressive, wind-blasted coastal overlook.

**Fort Ross State Historical Park** was established in 1906 to preserve the Russian settlement that arose in the early 19th century, with the help of native Alaskans. It has a forested area, lawns and coastal chaparral, with an informative visitor center, the original fort and a small cove beach.

The visitor center is well worth exploring, being a window to a time when part of California was a mix of Native American and Russian traders, before the Spanish, before the Yanks. The kayak on display if of the Aleutian Island type, meaning these Aleut people out of Alaska sure got around. Due to budget problems, Fort Ross was only open on weekends, but that might have changed. During the week, you can walk in and wander the grounds, but the visitors center was closed.

Another part of the park, a mile south of the visitor center is Reef Campground, closed in the winter, with 20 primitive sites strung down a wooded canyon, which protects it from the coastal winds. The canyon ends at a beach, making it a great place for inlanders to get away from both the heat and the crowds.

About three miles north of Fort Ross is **Timber Cove**. The Timber Cove Inn is somewhat fancier than the River's End, and it has a huge obelisk **sculpture by Benny Bufano**. It's a 93-foot piece of concrete, lead and mosaic titled The Expanding Universe, and it's only a few yards behind the inn. See www.timbercoveinn.com. The Timber Cove Inn is a complete resort, with lodging, meals and a full bar. This elegant inn and restaurant is set on a rocky point with really incredible ocean views. If you passed River's End and are now looking for lodgings, this would probably be the place, as there are few other places to stay in the area. The lunches are reasonable, and based on the superb fish tacos I had, well worth stopping for.

Look for Stillwater Cove Regional Park. Aptly named Stillwater Cove is a calm bay during summer months, perfect for swimming and launching a kayak. For kayaking, bring wheels, as it requires a short walk. Stillwater Cove Regional Park has pleasant camp sites and two or three miles of easy trails. I've recently heard that The Salt Point Lodge is closed. I can't be positive, so if you're hungry, at least slow down to look. The Ocean Cove Store, with a private campground, is also in the area.

Salt Point State Park consists of 6,000 acres of wooded uplands and coastal bluffs and coves. It features 109 camp sites, situated on both sides of the highway, along with miles of trails. For a short but impressive walk, hike down to Stump Beach, a deep, steep-sided cove fed by a small creek. A calm cove in summer, it can be a seething tumult in winter. Then cross the creek and hike the several miles of trails along the bluffs for continual spectacular ocean vistas.

Near the southern end of Salt Point State Park, around milepost 40.6, there is a long dirt shoulder and an emergency phone. Parking there gives you access to several miles of coastal bluff trails, with interesting rock formations and the rocky, not quite beach coastline so typical of Sonoma County. On the inland side is the trail to the Pygmy Forest, 1.8 miles inland.

Attached to Salt Point Park is **Kruse Rhododendron State Reserve**. Look for the turn off near the northern end of Salt Point. Drive about a mile, mostly on a dirt road, and there will be a spot to park six to eight cars. The Reserve sign is across the road, and the outhouses are a few yards down the hill. The five miles of trails in the 317 acre reserve range from the upland open forest with rhododendrons that tower over head to a deeply wooded canyon, complete with moss-covered redwoods and a thick carpet of fallen leaves. Try to save Kruse for the spring when the rhododendrons are in brilliant bloom.

The Sea Ranch is mostly a private colony, but there is a lodge, and there are five well-marked public access paths down to the beach or bluffs, with paved trails to rocky little coves and beaches. It's worth stopping and taking a walk along this scenic coast. You might even decide to buy a vacation house. Parking costs $6, and there is no parking on the road anywhere near these trailheads. The only places you can park for free are at the Sea Ranch Lodge and Restaurant and at the **Sea Ranch Chapel**. The sign for the chapel is hard to spot,  but at the same place there's a big fire truck sign with a picture of a fire truck on it. The chapel is just east of the highway, and it's absolutely lovely, worth stopping for a look or even a quiet meditation.

Sea Ranch ends just shy of the Mendocino County line at Gualala. The Mendocino part of Mendonoma stretches from Gualala to the Navarro River, a distance of another 40 miles. Along those miles are five communities, Gualala, Anchor Bay, Point Arena, Manchester and Elk. Point Arena is the only one you won't totally miss if you blink while driving through. But, just before crossing the river there's Gualala Point Regional Park, also a $6 parking fee. There are ample trails along the bluffs and down to the beach, the long sand spit south of the river mouth. There's also a campground, and the views from the bluff, looking over the river and town, are incredible. Note that the golf course on the other side of the fence is part of Sea Ranch.

The **Gualala Rive**r marks the county line. You can rent kayaks there (www.adventurerents.com), and a family campground is just up river on the Mendocino side. A sandy turnoff along the

highway takes you down to some parking near the river's mouth, places to launch a kayak or fish.

Gualala, in Mendocino County, is a good spot for art, food and beach combing. While in Gualala, visit one of the most interesting book and gift shops on the coast, **The Sea Trader,** on the ocean side of the

highway, just north of the main part of town. They have meditative music, new age books, crystals, decorative items, and, well the store is absolutely full of interesting items. Tell Kathy that I said to stop by. If you need a conventional bookstore, and every traveler needs books for those long nights in campgrounds or motels, the Four Eyed Frog is in the heart of town, on the inland side, in a small shopping center. Owned by two brothers, it's the only bookstore on this section of coast. Bones Barbecue, on the highway, is a good place for a quick meal.

Kathy recommends the Serenisea Cabins, between Gualala and Anchor Bay, as one of the better places to stay. Check them on the internet at http://www.serenisea.com/

She also recommends Trinks cafe, espresso and bakery in Gualala, a casual place to stop to eat or have a coffee. Kathy's been there for decades, so I trust her recommendations.

For the campers, Gualala Point Regional Park (707-565-2267), east of Hwy One, is located along the river, for your swimming and hiking pleasure.

143

At about milepost 2.77 you'll see a road heading toward the beach. It's called CR 526, not a great name, but in about a quarter mile you'll come to the **Bonham Trail**—named for local, Dee Dee

Bonham—which is a steep path down to a scenic little sandy beach, complete with driftwood and rocks just offshore.

About four miles north of Gualala, Anchor Bay is a similar small coastal town. Both Gualala and Anchor Bay can be driven through in a minute or two. It has lodging, such as Mar Vista Cottages (http://www.marvista-mendocino.com/, and there's a nice RV campground on the beach (707- 884-4222, abcampground@gmail.com).

For those who turned off back at Jenner and explored Duncans Mills, there's a delightful alternative to this rugged coastal road. About a mile east of Duncans Mills on 116, Cazadero Road turns away from the river and follows Austin Creek through six miles of steep-sided redwood canyon to the tiny village of Cazadero. About a mile before Cazadero is an absolute must stop. Raymond's Bakery (www.raymonds-bakery.com) is a destination for those who know the area. Besides delicious breads and other baked goods, they serve pizza, wine and beer. Sometimes on the weekends they have spontaneous music, depending on who walks through the door. While these sessions are rare in winter, they're quite common in summer. Hosts Mark and Elizabeth Weiss make even a total stranger feel like a regular. This is your alternative routh when the road north of Jenner washes out.

Cazadero is mostly a post office, church, hardware store and country store, a place to stop, get a snack and just enjoy the ambiance. Local crafter and columnist, Natasha Pehrson told me the area has more than its share of artists and musicians, and that people come from all over to enjoy the works of the creative locals.

Just past Cazadero there is an assortment of mountain roads, all of which eventually lead down to the coast at Fort Ross, Timber Cove, Stewarts Point or The Sea Ranch. I was talking with

144

a motorcyclist who was having a snack at the picnic bench beside the store. He'd ridden the back roads down from Gualala, and was making a day of winding through these scenic mountains. It's prime motorcycling country.

If you need to get back to Highway 101 and civilization, something I don't recommend, take Annapolis Road out of The Sea Ranch to Skaggs Springs Road, or take the road out of Stewards Point. Either way, you'll pass Lake Sonoma Recreational Area, after a long and winding road, before finding Highway 101 at Geyserville.

And herein lies the reason for the semi-deserted Mendonoma Coast. There are no direct roads back to 101 and all the main cities and freeways. Even 116 along the Russian River at the south end, is a fairly long drive through small towns. At the north end, 128, which follows the Navarro River before hitting Boonville in the Anderson Valley and then winding through another 50 miles of wine and pasture land, is a couple hours from Hwy. One to 101. Everything in between is mountain back road.

But, before we get lost, I believe I left you in Anchor Bay. The ten miles between Anchor Bay and Point Arena, are open and hilly, pastures, trees and ocean views. There are some stops along the way, the first is Schooner Gulch State Beach, a beautiful, day use only spot to picnic, relax and take a beach stroll. Should you stop here? If you are traveling through the Mendonoma Coast, you aren't in a hurry, so I suggest stopping. It's at milepost 11.30, and there's a sign that says to park facing south.

Just north of the trail down to Schooner Gulch, across from

Schooner Gulch Rd. is **another trail along the bluff leading to Bowling Ball Beach**, and you can guess what the rocks on the beach look like. It's a short walk, and just as you start, another trail runs off to the left to a restroom and then down to Schooner Gulch Beach. Take the right fork.

Trouble is, after going down some steps, the ladder down to the beach ends at some wet rocks, making the last few feet a scramble. Unfortunately, the rocks that give the beach its name are only visible at low tide.

The next access point is just south of Point Arena at Moat Creek, where there is a parking lot and a restroom. It's at about milepost 13. There's a very short hike down to a rock and driftwood-strewn beach, and there's a bluff trail that climbs above the

beach and runs about a mile down the beach, down to the area of Bowling Ball Beach. It's a beautiful walk, but don't get too close to the unstable bluffs.

**Point Arena** is the closest thing to a real town along the Mendonoma coast. It's actually an incorporated city, and at 473 people, California's smallest. Popular places to stay include Coast Guard House Historic Inn, The Wharf Master's Inn as well as at the lighthouse. There are also several restaurants in town, along with a fishing pier at the cove. Take Port or Iverson out off of Main (Hwy. One). The Pier Chowder House & Tap Room, my favorite, is there, along with the shops, coffee and a pizza place. You can also surf or launch a kayak or your fishing boat there. The cove is deep, and the north bluffs run all the way out to the lighthouse. The deep middle makes paddling out to the surf easy. Be sure to stop and tour the **Point Arena Lighthouse.** The road to the light is just north of town, and the lighthouse is set on a scenic, rugged tip of land that juts out into the sea. Tours, including the top of the light are $7.50, and you can also stay in the historic keeper's homes.

As you leave town, highway One turns left and becomes School Rd. for a bit. Park at City Hall, and behind the building you'll find a stile.

**Wander out along the bluffs** above the cove, then turn north and hike toward the lighthouse. There's one piece of land along the way that's still private, but a small group, not hunters or fishermen, likely wouldn't be bothered. However, this piece may soon be bought by BLM, making a stretch of awesome public land along over ten miles of bluffs, clear to Irish Beach. If you do this, be sure and look for the blow holes that blast you with air when waves surge through the caves below.

One real gem in Point Arena is the **B Bryan Preserve**, a private preserve housing majestic African animals in large open fields. Their motto is "Since when did your vacation help endangered species?" They have two guest cottages, a carriage house and tours each day at feeding time. The animals are wild and in large fenced fields, the cottages, hand built by Frank, the owner, are as charming as they are comfortable, with a double bed in the upstairs loft and two singles downstairs, a deck overlooking a small lake and a hot tub, all heated by solar power. There's even a dish and all the TV stations you could ask for. It's one of my favorite places to stay, and staying there helps them preserve these vanishing hoofed animals, which now include giraffes. You can contact them at **http://www.bbryanpreserve.com/** or by calling 707-882-2297.

Less than six miles north of Point Arena is the village of

147

Manchester. The road pulls away from the sea after the Point Arena Cove, but at Manchester, you can access the coast at Manchester Beach State Park. Sand dunes, five miles of

beach, a campground and usually lots of wind, make this a scenic walking and camping destination, but usually not too great for sunning. Since it's a state park, you can make reservations by calling (800-444-PARK). There are some environmental campsites, meaning a short walk and less demand, so you may be able to get in even during high season. There is also a KOA campground on the way to the state beach.

If you really need to get back to civilization, Mountain View Road is a 25-mile, very slow, winding road through the mountains and redwoods to Boonville on Highway 128. It is scenic, but by the time you get back, you will have forgotten why you needed to.

About another nine winding miles, with continual breathtaking coastal views, brings you to the town of Elk, a few homes and business along the highway. It's also the home of Greenwood State Beach, which requires a walk down a dirt road from the bluff to the beach, probably 200 feet or more below. There's a rest room at the top, and the beach is a good place to relax or fish. In summer, it's calm enough to launch a kayak, provided you are willing to drag it up and down the bluff. The charm here is the massive sea stacks in and around the cove. Like most of this section of coast, these stacks were carved by the violent waves that roar in during the winter storms. I never fail to stop and enjoy the view from the bluff, while I'm seldom tempted to walk down to the beach. Greenwood is a day use only beach, but there is lodging at Elk Cove Inn & Spa: http://www.elkcoveinn.com/. Rooms range from quite reasonable to fairly expensive, and the place is located right on the highway.

Leaving Elk, you twist and turn above disappearing and reappearing coastal vistas for another four or five miles, until you cross the Navarro River and hit Highway 128. This marks the end of the Mendonoma Coast and the start of the far busier and more populated Mendocino area. There are not a lot of attractions along the Mendonoma -Coast, few towns and some out of the way beaches. It's a get-away-from-it-all stretch of coast or a pleasant drive for those not in a hurry.

With Highway 128, a main access back to the busy world, a dividing line between two sections of coast, I have to add one more beach and place to camp. Navarro River Redwoods State Park: Navarro Beach. Just before crossing the River, Navarro River Rd. is a left turn, a narrow road that winds a mile or so down to a beautiful, wide beach, strewn with driftwood. Back against the bluffs there are ten camp sites. It isn't fancy, a place to park, pitch a tent and a picnic table and fire ring. Each site is semi secluded by tall shrubbery. There's an outhouse style restroom, and all the sites face the water. Even if you're not staying, it's a lovely place for beach lovers, and you can put a kayak or other small boat in the water near the mouth of the river.

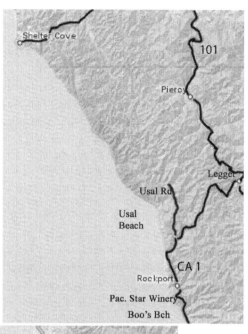

# The Mendocino Coast

Each summer I can hardly wait to load my kayak and pack my sleeping bag, because there's a piece of the Mendocino coast that offers, mile for mile, the richest variety of paddling and stunning scenery on America's West Coast. Only about 20 miles long, this rugged stretch of California holds at least a half dozen protected coves, four excellent state parks, sea caves and tunnels, great lodging and dining and four lush, wooded tidal rivers. Throw in entertainment and tourist attractions, and you have the perfect vacation.

For camping, kayaking and a romantic getaway, this is one of the best stretches of coast in California. If you've seen that delightful romance, "Same Time Next Year," with Alan Alda and Ellen Burstyn, their yearly weekends were at one of the lodges near Mendocino, and there are many of these, stretched along the highway, clustered around the village of Mendocino, all charming, most having great views of rocky coves. A quick look at http://www.mendocino.com/mendocino-hotels.html will give you a sample of the places to stay, although I'm still not sure which was used in the film.

Many of the places have restaurants attached to lodging, and Mendocino itself has loads of great places to eat, such as the MacCallum House Restaurant, in the heart of the village. Mendocino Hotel & Garden Suites at 45080 Main Street is a beautifully restored old hotel, and Main Street is the road that runs from Highway One  and along the bluff on the bay There are also a number of delightful little shops, jewelry stores and art galleries. In fact, some of the galleries alone are worth the drive.

The junction of the 128 and Highway One is about 145 miles north of San Francisco. The 128 meets the 101 at Cloverdale and winds through rolling hills and past Anderson Valley wineries, such as Handley Cellars, 3151 Hwy. 128 in Philo, a few miles past Boonville, which has wines so good, that when I stopped by with four friends, two joined the wine club. Check them out at: http://www.handleycellars.com/index.jsp.  Then it passes through

Boonville, home of Anderson Valley Brewing Co, a must stop for beer lovers. There is also Hendy Woods State Park, just off 128 and an ideal place to stop for a hike or a picnic. Then the road follows the Navarro River through a redwood forest and past Navarro River Redwoods State Park, Paul M Dimmick Campground. This campground, on the river, is in a beautiful, cool redwood grove, and it's only a few minutes from the coast. It's a good place to remember, as all the campgrounds along Hwy 1 on the Mendocino coast can be full at times during the summer, while Dimmick usually has room, but not showers.

Once on Highway One north of the Navarro, the next tidal river is the Albion. A very high bridge runs over it, and the quick  glance down is both rich with color and dizzying. On the north side, there's a steep road that leads down to the combination **launch, boat dock, RV campground** and fisherman's snack shop. Last time I was there it was five bucks to park and launch a kayak, but I don't know the cost for a regular boat. You can bring your RV and boat and spend  days fishing or exploring up river and out through the cove, past the mournful fog horn and along the convoluted coast.

If you boat up river, a smooth, blue-green liquid highway, in a short way you come to one of the most **memorable houseboats** you'll ever see. This is a houseboat as bizarre as anything from the golden days of Sausalito's floating shanty town. A great assortment of rotting logs and timbers holds up this piece of livable art. The sides are shingled on the first floor, many missing and revealing insulation. The second floor is mostly a collection of old wooden windows nailed together. Clothes are hung on racks in the upstairs rooms, and a small, vociferous herd of hostile terriers patrol the place. The house rides so low that the entrance is only inches above the water line. Yet people live there and are very protective of it. Signs warn trespassers to stay clear.

Farther up river there are a couple of more odd dwellings. Two tiny buildings float a few yards apart. One looks like an igloo and is apparently for storage. The other is just big enough for a single bed and a place to sit and read. Privacy comes in all shapes and sizes.

On my trip up the Albion, all signs of civilization ended at those two dwellings, except for a sign a mile or so up river that warned against trespassers. There wasn't a building or even a road in sight. Perhaps these owners were afraid that someone might land and pick a flower or put down their sleeping bag and spend the night in the lush, green meadows. Unfortunate, since the meadows along the river looked like great places to camp. I don't know how far a power boat can navigate the river, but a kayak can continue until the river loses itself in a thicket, probably a mile beyond where any other boat can venture.

Below the launch there is a long dock with boats tied up, mostly fishermen. It's easy to get out of the Albion, out under that fantastically tall bridge, past the rock with the fog horn, out where the cove gradually opens to the sea. Going straight out avoids running through the surf, at least in summer. Exploring the little beaches and side coves requires care, as each one is more exposed than the last, and paddling around a rock can put a kayaker face to face with breaking waves. This isn't a problem for boaters and fishermen, as they don't get close in against the rocks, but go straight out into open water. I took some friends out among the coves and when we went through an opening in the rocks, we encountered waves breaking almost against the cliffs. One friend was tossed out of his kayak, and it was a scramble to get back to protected water.

As you head north from the Albion, you start to see those lovely lodges and B and B's. In about four miles, you drop to the beach at Little River. Van Damme State Park is on both sides of the road. Inland, there's a nice, wooded campground with all the amenities you expect from a state park campground: nice campsites, hot and cold water, and real toilets, but usually full in summer.

The ocean side is also part of the park. Day use parking is free, but RV camping overnight costs, and with our park system, that cost can change at any time. The parking lot abuts a wide beach in a sheltered cove. Waves, inches high, lap the gravelly beach, and in the summer, particularly on weekends, you'll always see kayaks. It's one of the easiest places to launch and see sights you won't see many other places, such as a sea tunnel many yards long along the north wall of the cove. Even for people who normally don't kayak, a tour here is a must for travelers in the area.

For the summer traveler without a kayak on the car's roof, there is an outfitter in the area that provides tours. Lost Coast Kayak, a concession at Van Damme, runs two to three hour tours from the beach at Little River. Owner Jesse Spencer says, "Our season runs from May through October, but May and October are subject to cancellation depending on the weather." You can reach them at: http://www.lostcoastkayaking.com/.

Van Damme is an excellent state park, but it's very popular and very difficult to get into unless you make reservations a century or two before your planned visit. Sometimes, as in the other parks in the area, if you show up around 2:00 or 3:00 in the afternoon, there might be a cancellation. However, within blocks on either side of Little River there are many of those lovely lodges, most of them fairly pricy, but a few that are reasonable. Most of these places are on the internet, so click before you drive.

Two more miles up the road takes you to **Mendocino**. I think that for the general traveler this is a

great place to plant yourself for a few days. Centrally located on this section of coast, it has all the tourist amenities, walking paths along the bluff that are a huge draw for artists and photographers, a peaceful, old time pace of life and one of the best tidal rivers I've ever seen. There is even a really nice and quite popular beach at the foot of the bluff, at the beginning of town, one popular with both sunbathers and surfers.

If you stay, take a long walk along the headlands, take your camera, and if you are a couple, you'll have the urge to hold hands as you stroll. Also, if you are planning your trip in July, their annual music festival is a must: (http://www.mendocinomusic.com/?gclid=COeSo6mrm6oCFRxrg-

wod63R-wg). Big tents are erected on the bluff across from Main Street, and they have a great program each year.

**Big River** has a hotel, kayak rental and launch ramp on the south side. The north side, accessible from a road leading off Highway One, just north of the bridge, has a parking lot on the beach, a place to play in the water, to wander, or to **launch a kayak**. Once logging trucks rumbled up the dirt road on the north side of the river, and on one trip, my peaceful paddling was shattered by the sound of industrial logging less than a quarter mile from the river, a big conveyer hauling logs down a hill, like being inside a factory.

A few years ago the state purchased over 7,000 acres around the river, and now it's a serene

155

wonderland with trees arching over the river for eight miles, until a huge fallen redwood blocks further progress. If you want to canoe or take an outrigger, contact Tour Big River: http://www.catchacanoe.com/tourbigriver/index.htm

About a mile further north is another state park, **Russian Gulch**, not to be confused with the beach in Sonoma County. To me, this is the most scenic park in the area. The campsites are strung along the creek, under the shade of tall trees. At the end of the road that serves the campsites you can  pick up the Fern Canyon trail that leads through a damp, green forest to the Falls Loop trail and a waterfall, about an hour's walk each way. Walking down the creek for a few hundred yards takes you to the beach, located in a deep and totally calm cove. As you walk down the creek, keep your eyes open, as you just might see a family of river otters playing just a few feet from the path.

For the kayaker, this is another great place to launch. The  cove is deep and has **rocks and arches** to glide around and through. On the south wall of the cove, there is an almost magical sea arch that leads to the massive bay on the north side of the town of Mendocino.

About two miles north of Russian Gulch is the community of Caspar, the next place with a real beach, a great bathing beach and another place to launch a kayak. However the real draw in this small community is the Caspar Inn, a funky roadhouse about a block off Hwy. One. It's a hotel, restaurant and night club, and during the summer, they have music almost every night, often itinerant musicians who happen to be passing through. The rooms are

very inexpensive, $45 to $100, depending on who is playing that night, as room rate includes tickets to the show.

One can paddle out of the cove at **Caspar** and cautiously into the next cove south and look up at the **lighthouse.**

The only thing resembling a real city is four miles north of Caspar. Fort Bragg is the only town on Highway One—from where it diverges from the 101 by the Golden Gate Bridge, to where it reunites with the

101 around Leggett—that has chain stores, such as drug stores, coffee shops and supermarkets. At almost 8,000 people, Fort Bragg is the coast's major metro area. Many of the hotels, motels and restaurants even have wifi, including the wonderful Headlands Coffeehouse at 120 East Laurel in downtown. They have great coffee drinks and wonderful pastry. Around the corner on Highway One, the North Coast Artist Gallery, a cooperative, showcases some of the best of the local talent, and it's a place I picked up my favorite ceramic bowls and plates.

A couple of blocks north the North Coast Brewing Company is right on Highway One, just about across from the Skunk Train. I love brewpubs, and this is one of my favorites, as it has great ales and excellent food.

Just past the North Coast Brewing Company, take Elm Street toward the beach and look for Glass Beach, once a dumping ground for old bottles and trash, it's now part of MacKerricher State Beach and very colorful from all the tumbled beach glass.

And, speaking of the Skunk Train, also on the highway, this is a wonderful trip to do at least once. Actually they have two trips.

One that goes half way to Willits and returns, and the other that makes the full round trip between the two cities, almost 20 miles apart. It's a lovely excursion through the woods, with one long stop in the middle, and they give you a bit of time to grab a bite and look around Willits. If you like trains, and I suspect everyone does, take a few hours for a summer ride.

On the north side of the Noyo River, at the southern end of town, take a right on Harbor Drive and go down the hill to the harbor. It's a colorful place, with shops and lots of cute little seafood restaurants. Take a **stroll along the docks** and see the fishermen unloading their boats.

Looking down at the Noyo River in Fort Bragg some years back, I wondered where it wandered. I had my kayak on the car, as always when I'm traveling the coast. Not knowing where the boat ramp was, I drove down past the gift shops and sea food restaurants and out to the cove at the river mouth. As is typical in summer, the beach was gray and cold. I rode the plump, slow swells between the breakwaters and into the marina area.

There is a quality of rust and decay and submerged worlds at water level along a marina. The undersides of docks and piers have an art and history of their own. Remnants of metal and wooden structures hang down, and each surface is covered with the assortment of sea creatures that cling and wait for whatever meal floats by. Unidentifiable items bob in the dark green water, and various swimming creatures leave tiny wakes in the shadows. Life organizes itself in the under shadows much like it does on the docks above. This is a vivid memory from my paddle under the docks some years back.

Since that first trip, I discovered a public boat ramp and parking lot. It's a few blocks inland on Highway 20, which leads to

US 101 at Willits, and the inland terminus of the Skunk Train. From Highway 20, turn left on So. Harbor Drive, and right on Basin. There's a big public lot and a nice boat launch ramp you can drive right down to.

A short way up river from the ramp there's an interesting trailer park, with many coaches on the river's edge, with decks over the river and row boats, canoes or kayaks tied up in the back. If you go far enough up the river, you will cross the Skunk Train tracks and probably hear the train whistle.

There are motels and hotels along the highway in town, and there is also a strip of places on the north end of town, almost on the beach. These front the highway, but at the back, there's an old road, no longer open to cars, but used by walkers and bicyclists, and this road runs along the beach. In town there is no beach access other than Glass Beach and the mouth of the Noyo, so if you like beach walks, go north of downtown.

Also, just north of town is another state park, one with a marsh and pond to walk around and a nice beach. MacKerricher State Park has campsites I really appreciate. Each is set back between rows of thick and high shrubs, giving you the privacy that's lacking in most campgrounds. This is a place I've camped even during the busy season, by coming by in the early afternoon and checking for cancellations or early departures.

For surfers, look for the city limit sign at the north end of Fort Bragg and park in that big dirt lot. Cross the highway and follow the well-worn path to the beach. This is one of three or four good surfing spots along this coast. With all the rocky coves, surfing spots are at a premium. Another is at the mouth of Big River in

Mendocino and **Boo's Beach,** 15 miles north of Fort Bragg.

Be sure to pick up whatever you need in Fort Bragg, including gas, before you continue north. There's not a whole lot more until you hit the 101 at Leggett, some 43 miles up the road. However, there's still plenty to see.

There are a couple of accessible beaches above Fort Bragg, including one at MacKerricher State Park. No need to go through the main entrance. Go a bit further to Mill Creek Rd. and take a left. This will take you past the campground and to the beach parking lot. Another beach is right along the highway a few miles north.

About 12 miles north of Fort Bragg, at mile marker 73.58, and keep your eyes open for it, is **Pacific Star Winery**, my favorite winery. Owner and wine maker, Sally Ottoson, is a delightful person, a lover of the environment, a fountain of information for the area and a gifted wine maker. Add to that the location of the winery, perched on a windy bluff over a roiling sea, and you have a perfect stop. You can taste all her wines for $5, and I recommend "It's My Fault," a wonderful red blend. She also has a small deli case with cheeses and a few sandwiches. Tell her I sent you. You can call before you go: 707.964.1155

Once you've loaded your trunk with wine, drive a couple miles further, and as the road drops down to beach level, you'll see a dirt road leading off toward the beach. That's Boo's Beach, one of the best surfing beaches in the county. Don't be alarmed by the shark attack a few years ago. They don't like the taste of people, so it probably won't happen again. I used to love to camp at Boo's, but now they have that sign that seems to pop up everywhere these days: "No overnight parking or camping." Now you have to go a couple of miles further north to either the KOA or the state park campgrounds along the highway, neither of which are free, as Boo's used to be.

I've had some delightful nights at Boo's and have met some

interesting people. I recall one guy, 80 years old, staying in his camper. He didn't do the state parks, because they didn't allow dogs. He owned a business in Idaho and was a fisherman. He was working his way south to Baja, stopping along the way to camp, fish and whatever. I sat in his camper, drinking wine with him, talking and watching the moon over the water for hours.

While it's easy to ignore sleepy little **Westport**, don't. It's worth visiting, and it's a good place to stay, if you like quiet, out of the way places. You'd never guess that this tiny village was once the biggest coastal town north of San Francisco, beginning in 1877 as  Beal's Landing. A year later James Rodgers constructed a wharf, 20 feet wide and 375 feet long, extending out from the bluff and anchored to the rocks. You can still see the remnants of this. Look for the marker near the Westport Inn and Deli, and walk to the view point on the bluff. Freight was loaded and unloaded, carried on wagons inland, and there were six mills that were kept busy with local lumber. When the Skunk Train was completed from Fort Bragg to Willits, Westport started to decline. The last mill closed in 1920, and now it's just a quiet place for tourists who want charm and serenity.

If you decide to stay, and this is the last place on the coast for a very long way, I recommend the Westport Inn & Deli. Rates start at $70 + tax per night, single occupancy for charming cabins. The Deli, which serves breakfast and sandwiches looks more like someone's living room than a restaurant. Thelma and Otto Marsh have owned the place since 1972, and they love sharing the rich history of the place with visitors. If for some reason they are full, across the road and down a block is the Westport Hotel, a quaint old building.

If you are camping, there's a KOA near Westport, and there is a state park campground a short drive above Westport. The campground is on the ocean side, on the bluffs, and there are trails down to the beach.

Once you pass the campgrounds, there is nothing for 27 miles, until you connect with the 101 at Leggett, home of the drive through redwood, which costs $5. Actually, there isn't much in Leggett either, and you must drive quite a ways north on 101 before you find another town.

Unfortunately you've left the coast about 7 miles north of Westport, and there is only one alternative that keeps you close to  the coast, **Usal Road**. It takes off to the left shortly after Highway One turns inland. I've never been able to take it, as it is impassable much of the time, and at best it's a four wheel drive road. I was determined to try it last trip, but locals said there was no way, the folks who occasionally grade it hadn't yet, and even four wheel drive vehicles were getting stuck out there. On top of that, we had a freak very late rain, so nothing could get through. It's a one-lane road that eventually connects with Chemise Mountain Road near the road to Shelter Cove. If you are considering trying it, always check in with the locals. However, it is passable for five miles to the Usal Campground at the state park. With four wheel drive, on a good day, you might make it the whole way. Otherwise you don't see the ocean again until Shelter Cove, assuming you are willing to make another long drive.

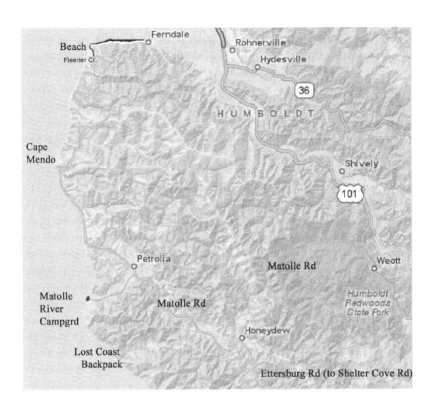

## The Lost Coast

In the last chapter I left you in Leggett, driving through a redwood tree. I apologize, as there isn't much in Leggett. In fact, as you turn north on US 101, there isn't very much for quite some time. However, if you like to camp in redwood forests, you will be in camper heaven. There are a number of parks and campgrounds on 101.

The 101 follows the Eel River, often in a rugged canyon, alternating between sections of freeway and wandering two lane road, passing through a series of parks and roadside attractions, such as the Grandfather Tree and the Log House. The gift shop inside a tree is closed, and Confusion Hill sits between Richardson Grove and Garberville. The first parks are Standish-Hickey State Recreation Area and Smithe Redwoods State Reserve. **Standish-Hickey** was one of the parks closed by the state, so the very small  local community, part of Mendocino Area Parks Association, took it over and are running it. It's a lovely park, less expensive than state parks and not crowded on recent visits. They have special rates for people with handicapped placards. This a labor of love for them, so do stay there on your travels. Also, Across the highway is the **Peg House** stoe and complex, walk up window, outside tables and the **best salmon sandwich** Iv'e ever had.

Soon you'll pass Richardson Grove State Park, which has been in the news as I write this. Caltrans wants to widen the highway through the park to allow long trucks to pass. You'll see, as you zigzag between the ancient giants on the narrow road, why the long trucks have trouble. I'd be nervous driving a large RV. Richardson Grove, however, is a wonderful park, located on the river, with many ancient redwoods and excellent camp sites. Then there is Benbow Lake State Recreation Area, and small resort community, named for the Benbow Lake along the highway.

Next you reach Garberville, the only real town along the Eel, and the old hippie capital of northern California, as well as the home of the Reggae Music Festival each summer, attended by thousands of young people in tie-dye clothing.

I think Garberville is a must stop. It's an interesting little town, and most of it is along Redwood Drive, the main road, which connects with 101 at each end of town. If you're hungry and want local color, try the Eel River Cafe on the east side of the street. It's a friendly place, and they put out a satisfying breakfast. A couple of blocks north and on the west side of the street is the Branding Iron Saloon. If you stop for a cold one, you'll get to know some locals and get a real feel for the town.

And here is where you need to make a decision. If you don't want to miss any of the accessible coast, you'll need to turn off to Redway, Briceland and Shelter Cove. And after making the 25 mile twisting, climbing and dropping drive to Shelter Cove, you'll know why so much of it is undeveloped.

Shelter Cove was a small fishing village, which grew into vacation homes plus a fishing village. Because the King Range is basically vertical, highway builders went inland, rather than try to put Hwy. One through the area. As a result, Shelter Cove is hard to reach by road, but people arrive by boat and by air. They have an airport. There is a marina and a launch ramp, sheltered by a short jetty, for fishing boats or kayaks. There's an RV park, half dozen places to stay and about that many places to eat. Since it snows in the King Range in the winter, I can't imagine anyone going to town unless they absolutely had to. However, if you're tired of the same old tourist spots, or if you are an ocean fisherman, try Shelter Cove.

The King Range, a wild, wondrous area, has loads of hiking trails. King's Peak Road is 17 miles from where you pick up the Briceland-Thorne Road at Redway (it becomes Shelter Cove Road). Turn right on King's Peak, Tolkan Campground is 3.5 miles, Horse Mountain campground is 6 miles. You can also turn left on Chemise Mountain Road, and go 2 to 3 miles to a campground I really like, Wailaki campground. It's a BLM campground, and it costs $8. Chemise Mtn. Rd. is paved, and there are plenty of sites, so you probably will get a space. It's nicely wooded, with large campsites.

If you are at Horse Mountain Camp, you can drive west on a primitive road, Saddle Mtn. Rd. to a Y. The left takes you up to Horse Mountain and some great views. The right takes you to the trailhead for the King Crest Trail. From there you can climb to King Peak (4,087 ft.) or continue to hike for miles or days through the wilderness.

However, the most popular trail is the Lost Coast Trail, which runs from the mouth of the Mattole River at Lighthouse Road to Shelter Cove. It's a 25 mile trek, mostly on the beach, on the only really wild and remote section of the California Coast. It's a three day trip. Yes, it's only 25 miles, but that's walking in the sand and arranging to hike one section only at low tide. There's a parking lot at the end of Lighthouse, and logically, you have a second car left in Shelter Cove. The drive back is much longer.

Once you've enjoyed **Shelter Cove,** drive back to around

Briceland, which really isn't a town, but you see a junction with Ettersburg Honeydew Rd., the road to both towns. The road doesn't actually pass through Ettersburg these days, it's on a side road, just a short detour, but the river is wide and slow and inviting at Ettersburg, a great place for a swim, but your destination is Honeydew. It's not that many miles, but like the road to Shelter Cove; it winds and twists, testing your resistance to motion sickness. It's a beautiful drive through the hills and mountains, but it feels like forever before you drop into Honeydew.

166

**Honeydew** isn't actually a town either. It's a store and a few houses scattered around. The important thing about Honeydew is that it's a junction. To the right is another road to the 101, and to the left is the way to the Mattole

River, Petrolia, Cape Mendocino and a rarely visited section of the coast, including one of my two all time favorite campgrounds.

But first, for the traveler who didn't turn off at Garberville, but opted to continue to Humboldt Redwoods State Park, the Avenue of the Giants, the cute, woodsy towns of Myers Flat and Weott, you must stop at Humboldt Redwoods State Park, with the largest old-growth redwood forest that has not been logged. Even if you don't have a lot of time, hike the Rockefeller Loop Trail/Bull Creek Flats (ADA Accessible) for a half mile that rivals the Lady Bird Johnson Grove. This loop trail is near where Bull Creek meets the South Fork Eel River. Trees soaring to immense heights combined with a relatively open understory give you the real old-growth forest experience. The trailhead is 1.1 miles west of the Avenue of the Giants on Bull Creek Flats Road (becomes Mattole Rd), which breaks off at Avenue of the Giants mile marker 20.6, at Dyerville. You access this from Avenue of the Giants, rather than 101 along this stretch.

Now here's the alternate route to Honeydew. You've turned on Mattole Road off the 101, stopped at Humboldt Redwoods State Park, perhaps taking a hike in the Rockefeller Forest (highly recommended by Sally at Pacific Crest Winery). Now you are in for another of those wild and wonderful roads. It's 23 miles to Honeydew, over the mountain, and if you tell me you did it in less than an hour, you're probably the kind of person who claims he caught an 18 lb trout. You are entering the Lost Coast, and everything here takes much more time. If you were in a hurry, you'd be on the 101, heading toward Eureka.

Once you get to the top, there's a view of the Mattole Valley, far below, that absolutely needs to be taken in. Pull over, get out of the car, grab your camera and take a few minutes to be awestruck.

You've been on Mattole Road for between an hour and an hour and a half, and now you're in Honeydew. Get out, stretch, buy a snack or a soda and get ready for another 15 mile drive along the Mattole to Petrolia. This isn't a highway or even a first-class road, so it's going to take at least a half hour. If it's summer, look for a place where you can walk down to the Mattole River. It's very warm in summer and there are some nice swimming holes, where you might even meet a friendly garter snake, as I did once.

On the way to Petrolia, you'll pass **A.W. Way County Park,** on the river, where camping is $20 per night. No reservations, so you probably won't have a problem just showing up. This park is 7.5 miles from Petrolia.

What's in Petrolia? A few houses, and I think there's a small convenience store, but businesses come and go around here. It is, other than Shelter Cove, the only other town on the Lost Coast. It sits just north of the Mattole River, five miles from the beach. Just before crossing the river and entering the town, turn left on Lighthouse

168

Road. and go five miles (the last two being dirt and gravel) to **Mattole Campground**, a BLM site, with an $8 camping fee. It's right against the beach dunes, among the huge, scenic chunks of driftwood. Just outside the campground is the parking lot for the Lost Coast hike to Shelter Cove.

Once this place was rarely visited. My first stay, summer of '94, there was only one other camper. A few years later, I had two neighbors. This summer it was more than half full. What's more, the wonderful sign is gone. There used to be a sign, with drawings of the local birds and marine mammals. The inscription said, "We love our beach; please take care of it." Below the inscription, it was signed by all the second and third graders at Petrolia School. It was probably the most touching thing I've ever seen, and it brought tears to my eyes. How could you not love a place that's been adopted by a group of trusting, caring children?

Imagine a clean beach, no fast food wrappers, and no cigarette butts. Imagine a beach where you can walk for miles and feel like you are the last person on the planet. This is it. The millions of people packed into California are somewhere else, and as you walk this beach, you could care less where they are or what they're doing. The only sounds are the waves and the sea birds. Peace and solitude!

But civilization calls again, along with the necessities of travel, food and gas. And I hope you filled up in Garberville or Shelter Cove, because none of these towns have a station. You're next gas is in Ferndale, 30 miles and at least an hour away.

There are drives that will take your breath away and that you'll remember for life: Yosemite Valley, the Big Sur Coast, the rim of the Grand Canyon, Zion Canyon, the Amalfi Coast in Italy and the road from Petrolia to Ferndale. If this road were food, you'd gain twenty pounds on the drive. It's 30 almost-deserted, magical miles, four to five of which are along the beach.

You leave Petrolia and wind along the rolling landscape, pastures and grassy hillsides, and soon the road hits the coast. There is a four to five mile stretch where the road runs right along the beach, the only spot for many, many miles in either direction. As you hit the coast, the road crosses a small creek/gulch. Just on the other side, there is room to park a few cars, and there's a stile in the fence. It's one of the few places to access the beach.

About a mile or more further, the road is right along the beach, and there is no fence for some distance. At an outcropping of rock, there's a short path from the edge of the road to the rocky beach. This is access, and the rocks keep the small summer waves from breaking, so it's a place to launch a kayak. You will then have over **fifty miles of the Pacific Coast** all to yourself.

Soon, there is a strip of grassy meadow between the road and water, and cattle graze there, and it's fenced. No more access. Just before the road turns abruptly inland and steeply upward, you reach Cape Mendocino, which is a strange name, considering you've been in Humboldt County for the last fifty miles. Beautiful Sugarloaf Island sits just offshore, and if you're a surfer, you see nicely shaped waves breaking next to Sugarloaf. However, it's fenced off with no trespassing signs, but I've seen surfers out there before. I'm guessing that if you're a local or if you ask really nicely at the ranch house a couple hundred yards south, you might, and I emphasize "might" get permission to surf there.

Cape Mendocino with **Sugarloaf Island** is impressive to come upon; more so if you are traveling south and come down that steep road, round a bend and look straight down on it.

We once bought a woodcut at an art fair, a piece by Lisah

Horner, a Berkeley artist. She was going to ship it, and it took a very long time. When it arrived, there was a note of apology, saying she'd mislaid the order. To make things right, she included another woodcut, which I recognized immediately, Cape Mendocino, looking down from the north. I contacted her and found it's also one of her favorite places.

Slow, winding, deserted, lush, magnificent and undulating are just a few of the words that come to mind when I think of the road from the cape to Ferndale. The road twists upward to a ridge with views in any and all directions, and then it drops down to cross the Bear River, through a ranch with the greenest fields I've ever seen, and rising again to another ridge.

At one point, you can pull over and look down at the mouth of the Eel, several miles north, and then the road twists along the ridge again, through woods and displays of vivid wildflowers, even in summer, before finally dropping quickly into the Victorian wonderland known as Ferndale. You can get gas and food in Ferndale, and you can find lodging. It's a picturesque little town, and the main road is lined with Victorian buildings painted in all those bright colors with the fancy trim. From here you can easily connect

to the 101, via route 211, about five or six miles. Eureka is twenty miles away, only a half hour. If you want quiet and cozy, find lodging in **Ferndale.** If you want tourist amenities, go on to Eureka or its neighbor, the university town of Arcata. If you wish to stay, the Shaw House Inn on Main Street is a charming and popular B and B. Ferndale has some really interesting little shops to explore.

But, I've promised to get you to the beach, and there are not that many places around here, so in the center of town, go west on Centerville Road for about five miles to a stretch of beach usually only enjoyed by locals. The ride out is charming, and there's a pond along the way, near the beach. When you first hit beach there's parking for several cars by cement barriers that are covered with graffiti, but the real gem is a short drive further south and up. **Fleener Creek Overlook** has a trail head down to a driftwood-strewn beach. It's a half mile trail and several hundred feet down. This is a transition area, where the lost coast meets civilization. Walk down the trail and beachcomb alone below the towering bluffs. Once you've enjoyed Ferndale, visited the beach, had a meal, perhaps stayed the night, you have left a very special section of coast behind, and are ready to rejoin 101, which follows the coast the rest of the way to Oregon.

However, there's one little transition area, not Lost Coast, but not part of the 101 strip, so let's take a side trip before we rejoin the rest of California. The mouth of the Eel River is a beautiful, lush and off-the-beaten-track place to visit, so when you take the 211 to Fernbridge, turn left, avoid the freeway and continue north on Eel River Drive to Loleta, a very tiny, very old town with a few businesses on the one block downtown. The one destination in Loleta is the cheese factory, with tours and tastings.

As you go through town, you'll see Cannibal Island Road, a left turn. It heads straight toward the coast. Keep going a couple miles to Cock Robin Island Rd. and turn left. Just before the road goes over a one-lane bridge, there's a parking lot with the Pedrazzini boat ramp where you can launch your fishing boat, canoe or kayak. It's about a mile up from where the river meets the ocean, so it gets rough to the west. Going up river is a delight, as there are no obvious signs of civilization, just a thick, green riparian corridor with lots of birds and no human sounds. There are miles of waterways to explore up river.

You will probably be the only one in the parking lot on any
172

given day, unless it's warm and not windy (rare). You can also cross the bridge, and part of the island is a wildlife area, the other being private land.

Back on Cannibal Island, you can continue west for another mile to the end of the road at Crab Park. There's room for a half dozen cars. The beach is in the lagoon at the mouth, and the entrance to the Eel is just over the lagoon and down the beach. You can wander the beach dunes or huddle up by a beach fire as the three teen girls were doing on my last visit.

Several areas from the **mouth of the Eel** to the south jetty of Humboldt Bay and near 101 are part of the Eel River Wildlife area, something worth exploring.

Now go back up Cannibal Island Road, almost to Loleta and turn left on Duncan Road. A very short drive will take you to Copenhagen Road. Turn left again and continue on for about four scenic miles until it dead ends at Hookton Road/Table Bluff Road. Turn left, and very shortly you'll be back at the coast, at the south spit of Humboldt Bay, a 5.5-mile sandspit that ends at the jetty at the entrance to the bay.

The trip out to the south jetty is a different experience than in the mid 90's. On my first trip I wrote about encampments, not weekenders in tents and R.V.s, but old buses, cars, lean-tos, and tent complexes, places that looked like squatters' camps, and seedy people with weasel glances that spoke of desperation and territorialism.

Returning in 2011, it is now the Mike Thompson Wildlife Area, named for the environmental congressman. Beach goers, nature lovers and fishermen now wander the inviting dunes, rather than face the intimidating looks of the former residents. It now has a gate that closes at dusk, preventing the campers from returning. Something important is won, while something is lost. It's a win for nature, public access and a clean environment. However, something dark, dramatic, oddly seductive and very human has been

173

lost, that outlaw life that many of us have flirted with at some point in life. I can relate to both visions, as someone who has been progressing from outlaw to respectable camper over the last couple of decades.

The weather fit both visits. The first time it had been blowing fog, Eureka virtually invisible across the bay. This time the sun was shining, Eureka and Arcata stood out on the far shore, and people were enjoying the beach, fishermen on the jetty sharing fishing stories with me. It was a cleaner and happier public beach, and one worth visiting for any beach lover or fisherman.

To get back to the main highway, go back Table Bluff, which becomes Hookton Road and keep going away from the ocean. Just before you reach 101, stop at the Humboldt Bay National Wildlife Refuge. You'll see signs. Part of this is along Hookton Road, and there's a parking lot right off the road at **Hookton Slough,** and there's a dock to launch a boat from, to explore the refuge. The main visitor center is just north of the junction of

Hookton Road and Eel River Drive, just before the freeway. It's a great place to see wildlife, such as deer, herons and possibly coyotes. There are some nice, flat hiking trails, and well worth a hour or so of exploration.

So, now you hop on the 101, heading north to Eureka and the next leg of your adventure.

174

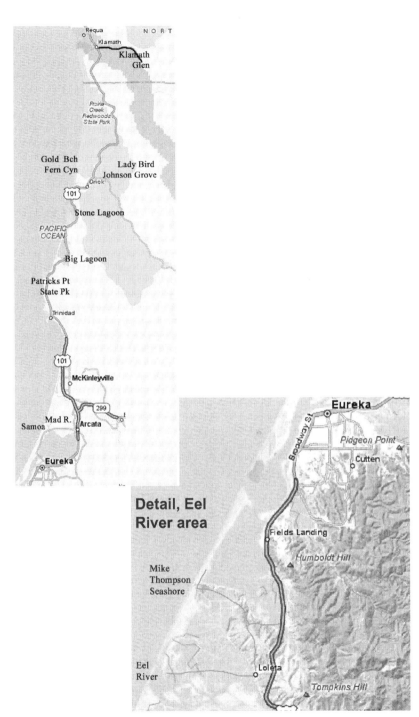

Detail, Eel
River area

# Humboldt Coast

In the last chapter, I left you finally reaching the freeway after spending a day or two semi lost on the Lost Coast. Now, you're probably anxious to get to Eureka and its wide assortment of restaurants, motels and shops, but there's a stop on the way that shouldn't be missed.

You may recall a contentious issue from the late 90's regarding Headwaters Forest. MAXXAM Inc., a company run by Charles Hurwitz, bought Pacific Lumber, a company that had run a sustainable timber business for a century. To pay off the investment, MAXXAM started clear-cutting everything in sight. Huge protests, tree sits and major publicity finally lead to a deal where the feds (and I think also the state) bought a piece known as Headwaters Forest. Now it's public land and well worth visiting. This is old growth, never-logged land, surrounded by denuded parcels, and the contrast is striking.

When I hiked in, it was from the trailhead in Fortuna, the shorter trail, which is now only open to BLM-guided hikes by reservation. The northern portion is open from dawn to dusk for anyone willing to make the 11 mile round trip. About six miles south of Eureka, you'll see Elk River County Road. Drive the five or six miles in to the trailhead and make a day of it. Don't worry; there are plenty of places to stay and eat in Eureka.

One striking thing I remember about this old-growth forest was that I couldn't see the forest floor, several feet below me, covered by centuries of accumulated detritus. The trees ranged from ancient giants to saplings, and as a gentle rain started, we sat in a hollowed-out tree many centuries old and watched the drops work their way through three hundred feet of leaves and needles.

That's a long hike, and now you need a city. Eureka, in recent years, has started to look like most cities, particularly as you enter from the south. There are the shopping malls and big box stores. There are also some of the better motels and hotels. However, downtown still has the individual flavor that makes it a nice place to visit. As you get into downtown, 101 separates into two one way streets, 5th goes north, 4th, south.

Letter streets cross the numbered streets, and historic old downtown is between C and K and from 4th down to the water. The center of old town is **2nd and F,** and old town is a really cool place, with great shops and places to eat, many situated in restored old Victorian buildings. Note that 4th is less nice, mainly motels, banks, professional buildings. 5th looks a bit seedy, and a few blocks east gets you

into residential neighborhoods. The motels along 4th and 5th are inexpensive to moderate. On my last visit I found a very cheap place (travel writers are not terribly well paid), but I won't recommend it because of the strange people wandering around in the middle of the night, making noise, singing loudly and acting the way people who live in cheap motels act.

I love brewpubs. I love pub food, and I love microbrew ales, so whenever I'm in a town with a brewpub, I always stop to eat and drink. On 4th between G and H is the Lost Coast Brewery, always fun, always packed. OK, they're 50 miles from the actual Lost Coast, but after two pints you'll forgive them.

Around the corner on F, between 2nd and 3rd is one of the places I love to stop and shop, Old Town Art Gallery. It's a cooperative gallery that's been around for thirty some years. I still love the painting I bought there fifteen years ago at a bargain price. Across the street and down on the corner is Many Hands Gallery, with a wonderful mix of handmade gifts, ceramics and more kinds of goodies than I can list. The store is packed with treasures. I can't remember everything in Many Hands, but I saw handmade ceramic coffee mugs for ten bucks less than any other place I've been. In the same block you'll see the American Indian Art and Gift Shop.

On 2nd you'll find Booklegger, stuffed with new and used books, and Eureka Books is the store for new books. There's also

177

Ciara's Irish Shop and Hurricane Kate's: dining with a twist. Stop in and find out what world fusion food is like. And, if you want to stay in old town in one of the Victorian buildings, there's Charter House Inns on 3rd and L.

Go down to the foot of F, and there's a walkway, a promenade that runs along the water for several blocks. There are some businesses accessible from the promenade, and the MV Madaket Bay Cruises leaves from there. Humboldt is a big, interesting bay, so stop in and ask about the cruise. As you stand at the dock at the end of F, you'll see **Woodley Island** just over the channel. There's

a marina there, and you can get to it by driving 101 to the north end of downtown and swinging left onto Hwy. 255 toward Samoa. Woodley is the first turn off.

If you're staying in town, you'll want breakfast, and I can recommend Kristina's at 250 W. 5th, which is where the 101 becomes a two way road.

Take the 255 bridge at the northern end of town to Samoa, on the north spit of the bay. Turn left at the stop sign and turn left again at the sign for the famous **Samoa Cookhouse**, the ultimate in

family style dining. They open the doors for meals, and you file in, grab a seat at one of the long tables, and they bring out each course in huge bowls and it gets passed along. Everyone should eat there once.

Oh, yes, while on the north spit, out near the Cookhouse, there are miles of public beaches out there if the weather is inviting enough.

Rather than go back to the 101 for the short drive to Arcata, home of Cal State Humboldt, since you are on the north spit, go back past the 255 to Samoa Blvd. which will take you over the **Mad River Slough** to Arcata. Note the lumber mill along the

slough, and note next to the road on the north side, a place to park a few cars and put in a kayak. Anyway, if you are a kayaker, note that, it's a lovely and scenic paddle through some winding wetlands.

Otherwise, continue on Samoa Blvd., and turn left on G. In four blocks you'll be at the Arcata Plaza, the hub of town. Find a parking place and take a walk. Most of the places to check out are on or near the plaza, including two really great bookstores, coffee places, shops, restaurants and the like.

While most of the motels are further north, near the 299 junction, the Lady Anne Victorian Inn is just four blocks from the plaza, at 902 14th street (www.ladyanneinn.com).

Take 11th or 14th east, up the hill for a few blocks and visit the Arcata Community Forest. That's right; some towns have a city park, Arcata has a city forest. You'll probably share the paths with university students.

There aren't many roads that offer a direct route inland, but the 299 is one of them, linking Arcata to Redding, along the Trinity River. But assuming you are staying on the coast, your next stop, and I hope you're hungry and thirsty, is McKinleyville.

Just past the 299 and over the Mad River, exit Central Avenue, and very quickly you'll see Six Rivers Brewery on the right. Like most brewpubs, it has good food and good ales. However, stay away from the flavored ales, either too sweet or too hot, and stay with pales, ambers, IPA and lagers. If you've had too many beers or just feel like spending the night, right across the street is the Sea

View Cabins at $95 per night. While there, check out Blake's Books in the heart of town. Always have a book on the ready when you travel.

Compared to Arcata and Eureka, there isn't much for the traveler in McKinleyville. However, there is a beach and a beach campground. Clam Beach County Park, at the north end of McKinleyville, and just before Little River State Beach has camping on the beach for $15. It's a wide and wide open beach, and day use is by donation.

As you pass the wide **Little River State Beach**, the coast becomes obscured by trees for a couple of

miles, and then you see the sign for Trinidad and Trinidad State Beach. The state beach doesn't have a campground, but there's an RV park in town, and Patrick's Point State Beach, just up the road, has camping.

Trinidad is a cute little beach town and fishing village. You can drive right down to the beach on Trinidad Bay to launch a boat or kayak, and there's also a launch ramp. The bay is fairly calm, fronted by high bluffs, topped with lovely homes. There are lots of sea stacks and rocks in the bay, some with miniature forests on top. I've kayaked Trinidad a couple of times, and it's fairly protected water two miles out to a point with lots of rocks. Past the point it's more open as the bay opens out to Little River Beach. The bay on any sunny summer day is filled with fishing boats and kayaks. There are also opportunities to learn rock climbing in Trinidad.

As you drive into town on Main Street, you'll see most of the town. There are two casual places to eat: Trinidad Bay Eatery and Beachcomber Cafe. The Emerald Forest has cabins, RV park and campground, something for everyone, including wifi. You can also stay at Patrick's Point Inn, Trinidad Inn, Ocean Grove Lodge and Hidden Creek RV Park. There's even a Native American Casino and a wine tasting room. However, a local insisted that the twisty road down to the casino isn't advisable for RVs. I never visit casinos, so I can't comment. Anyway, all of this is within a few square blocks.

From Main Street, you'll go left on Trinity Street and head down toward the water. Once down at beach level, there's a large parking lot. The bay with launching is on the south side of the lot and a small but very scenic cove public beach with small surf in summer is on the north. Looking west and up, you see **Trinidad Head,** and the trail starts at the parking lot. The trail, actually a

road, climbs for a bit and then splits into a loop. Go either way and you'll end up where you started. The views are spectacular from up there: the ocean, the bay, the beach, the town. Also up on the head is the historic lighthouse, standing high above the bay. Trinidad head is a popular hike with locals, and many walk their dogs there on a regular basis. There are also hiking trails along the bluff and down to the beach at Trinidad State Beach.

It's a pretty little town, a place that always makes me feel good to visit, and I'd never pass that way without having lunch or kayaking or just hiking up to the lighthouse.

From Trinidad you can get back on 101 or take Trinity Street to Stagecoach Road and drive along the state beach to

Patrick's Point Drive. There's also an exit off the highway for Patrick's Point. Patrick's Point Inn and Sounds of the Sea RV and Spa are on this road, almost to Patrick's Point State Park.

Patrick's Point State Park is a great place to camp. There are trails out along the rocky point, and you can hunt for agates on the beautiful beach. However, since it's a state park, they do take reservations, so there might not be space for the casual, drop-in camper. Still, one day I lucked out. Turns out that some university group had reserved the group campground, and after chatting with the nice researchers, they invited us to pitch our tents. It never hurts to strike up a conversation and to ask.

There are also environmental campsites at Dry Lagoon, which is like a marshy meadow, between Big Lagoon and Stone Lagoon, just north of Patrick's Point. You can register for these at Patrick's Point. Environmental camps mean you walk in, and you probably have to bring your own water, but most have portable toilets. There is also a nice beach at Dry Lagoon, a popular surfing spot.

You no sooner get back on the highway north out of

Patrick's Point when you approach Big Lagoon, 3.5 miles long, over 2 miles wide, with 18 miles of shore line. You can drive in on **Big Lagoon** Park Road. It's a county park with a nice beach with both ocean and lagoon access right at the parking lot, and the parking is $2 per day. There's also a campground for $20 per night. During the summer there are kayak rentals on the beach right by the end of the lagoon. Kayak Zak is based in Orick and has had kayak trailers both at Big Lagoon and Trinidad during the summer. If you don't see them, check Stone Lagoon. You can rent them on the spot, and the lagoon is calm water, or you can contact them at www.kayakzak.com. There is also a place to launch a boat into Big Lagoon right on 101,

just up the road. There is an interesting creek feeding Big Lagoon near the campground, a place to paddle and view wildlife. Harry A. Merlo State Recreation Area is another Big Lagoon place to launch your boat.

**Stone Lagoon** is a bit more than half the size of Big Lagoon, but still big enough for boating and kayaking. Look out from the parking area by the visitor's center, and see what looks like a curve in the far shore, about a mile and a half away. That's a boat in only campground. The state closed it because they couldn't afford to maintain it. However, it will soon open again, as Kayak Zak has taken over the closed visitor's center and will maintain the camp. Stop, as Kayak Zak is the place to learn about all the great places to paddle or to join a tour. However, if you paddle out and camp on Sharp Point, secure your food, as bears do visit the area. You can also turn left at the north end of Stone Lagoon at State Park Road for day use and a great place to launch a kayak or canoe.

The next lagoon is Freshwater Lagoon, which is on the inland side of the highway, and runs right along it. There's a wide shoulder on the ocean side for day use beach lovers to park. There used to be overnight camping for RVs, but, like most places on the coast, that's gone. Since you probably don't want to run across a busy federal highway carrying your boat, you can drive down to a short dirt road that runs between the lagoon and the highway, accessed from the north end of the lagoon. Trouble is, there's a small but sharp drop from pavement to dirt, and since I have a low clearance, passenger vehicle, I didn't want to take a chance on losing my exhaust system. It should be no problem for a pickup truck or SUV. It's a calm lagoon, and there appears to be something like a resort across the water.

If there's a town that fairly shouts "North Coast" louder than Orick, I've yet to see it. This wide spot along the highway sits at the entrance to Redwood National Park. I was so afraid the town was dying a few years back, as it seems half the businesses were up for sale. However, it looks like the town is doing OK for now. There are some stores, gas, restaurants and my favorite motel.

The **Palm Motel and Cafe** is on the left if you're headed north. It's nothing fancy, but the rooms are comfortable, clean and inexpensive. They have a pool, if it's ever warm enough to use it. Connected with the motel is the Palm Cafe, serving breakfast all day. This is a family run place, with real home cooking. If you are like me, when you travel, you want to get a feel for the area, sample the local color, rather than stay in some cookie cutter chain. The Palm Motel is as local color as you can get.

Redwood National Park has miles of trails running in and out of the mountains and down to the shore. Some trails extend 3 to 6 miles, but if you want to really taste the best of the redwood forest in one mile, drive up Bald Hills Road, just north of town about three miles to **Lady Bird Johnson Grove**. There's a sign along the highway, so you really can't miss it. When I first saw the sign, I figured, rightly, that if they were going to name a grove after a president's wife, it would be the most scenic in the park. True. It's a wide, well main-

184

tained loop trail, passing through rhododendrons that hang over your head, rich with blossoms and between massive giant redwoods that were already ancient when the first Europeans set foot on North America. There are ferns you can walk under, and the muted light creates an almost mystical experience. The area also has trails leading off from the loop, in case you want to do some serious hiking, one heading back down to the highway.

If you have nerves of steel and lots of extra time on your hands, continue on Bald Hills Road over the mountain to the Hoopa Valley Indian Reservation, where you can cross the bridge, pick up Highway 96 and follow the Klamath River to the Trinity, back to 299 and then back to Arcata. I say "nerves of steel" because Bald Hills is very narrow, very winding and also a logging road. These trucks roar down that road as if it were the interstate, and when you hear the roar, look for a place to pull over.

This park has kind of a strange arrangement, as Redwood National Park somehow shares space with Prairie Creek State Park. It's all the same scenery, thick groves of 300 foot redwoods, little streams and dozens of trails leading off in all directions. You can only tell which park you're in by watching the signs.

 There is a place where you can get off the 101, at Newton B. Drury Scenic Parkway, and you don't want to stay on the straight, boring highway. Just after exiting on Drury, you'll pass through Elk Meadow, where everyone, and I mean everyone, stops to photograph the **Roosevelt Elk.** They are wandering around just yards from the road, lots of cows and a few bucks with huge antlers. If you miss them at Elk Meadow, spend the night at Elk Meadow Lodge and watch the herd from your cabin window. At Davison Road, there's a parking lot for elk viewing and a visitor center, along with trailheads. It is also the entrance to Prairie Creek Redwoods State Park's Gold Bluffs Beach Campground (25 sites), with water, restrooms and wood. Sites are $20, and a sign at the beginning of the road will tell you if the campground is full, saving you an eight

mile drive on a dirt road. However, even if you can't camp there,

drive out to the parking area and hike **Fern Canyon**, a mile long box canyon, with 50 to 80 foot walls covered in ferns. You can also hike out of the canyon and into the redwoods for a loop back, or you can even access it on a longer hike from Drury Parkway. Just look for the trailhead sign. This is a popular hike, and being in a state park, the trails are well maintained and clearly signed.

The campground is on the beach, so there is no shade, and if it's windy, you have to deal with the sand. However, in nice weather, it's a superb place to camp, given the access to great hikes and an uncluttered beach.

As you are driving along Drury Parkway, you'll see signs saying "Trailhead 750 feet." There are lots of these, and it doesn't matter which one you take. It's one big, thick, primal forest, and it's all worth walking for three hours or even ten minutes.

Just before you get to the north end of Drury Parkway and exit the park, there's a left, Coastal Drive, which takes you along the bluffs over some fairly remote beaches. It eventually ends at Klamath Beach Road, but there are two forks further up, the left one staying along the bluffs to the mouth of the Klamath River is a good dirt road. The other is mostly paved and drops you a mile or two from the river's mouth. However, once on this road, you've left Humboldt County and entered Del Norte County, the subject of the next and last chapter.

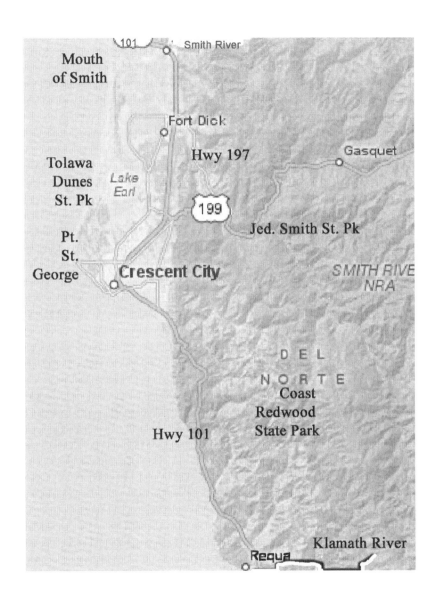

# Del Norte Coast

Shortly before running into the mouth of the Klamath, you crossed into the northwestern most county in California, Del Norte (don't pronounce the final e). It's a county of mountains, redwoods, foggy coasts and our first and best Wild and Scenic River. It's a county short on population, long on scenic wonders.

Let's get oriented. There is a road down both sides of the Klamath. When you come out of Redwood National Park and hit the river, you are on the Yurok Indian Reservation. They're good people, avid fishermen, and they love their land, so treat the area with respect. I've sent you out Coastal Drive, which means you are looking at the mouth of the river. There's a long sand spit on the south side, and you can walk out to where the river empties to the sea, where you can walk the beach, fish or surf. This is a place to fish for salmon and a good surf spot, if you don't mind sharks.

Right down from the hill at the junction of Coastal Drive and West Klamath Beach Road, nestled in the trees, is a Yurok outdoor gathering arena.

Take a **peek through the trees,** but don't disturb.

About 1000 feet back toward the highway on West Klamath, there are places to park along the road, right next to the river. Look carefully and you'll see a very short track, just wide enough for a car to back down and launch a small boat or kayak. It's only 20 or so feet down to the water. This is a little side channel, off the main channel and the wide mouth area. It's lush and green and, being off to the side, is pretty much immune to tides, currents and wind. It intersects with the main river, which has a current that gradually dies out as the mouth spreads out by the sand spit. If you

188

are a kayaker or small boater, and you've driven out there anyway, might as well put in and explore. Next to the Sacramento River system, the Klamath is the biggest in California.

As you drive back toward 101, some three or more miles back, Redwood National Park will be on your right, the Yurok reservation on your left. Also, you'll see the Klamath River RV Park, on Klamath Beach Road, near the 101, right on the river, a popular place for fishermen.

Once back on 101, turn left and go over the river. That little town, Klamath, is on the reservation. See Route 169 heading off to the right? Take that about three miles to Klamath Glen, then in two places where the road bends sharply, go right, and you'll end up at Roy Rook Launch. There's parking and a ramp. If you have a power boat, as in fishing, no problem with the current, but if you're launching a human powered boat, make sure there's another vehicle down near the mouth, as you can't fight the current. Just go with it for six miles of river though a steep sided, forested landscape.

But, before you do that, you best check out the take out point. Go back to the highway, turn right, and 101 follows the river through Klamath. When you get to Requa Road, turn left. I know you've just passed some pleasant looking RV parks and are tempted to stop, but trust me, go out Requa Road and you'll have two choices of places to stay. At the intersection of Requa and Mouth of Klamath Road is the Historic Requa Inn. And one look will tell you it's both historic and appealing. The rates (2011) Kings, Queens, Fulls, some with river views: from $89 to $179- season is May 1- Sept 30, off-season Oct. 1- April 30, www.requainn.com (707) 482-1425. Ok, there's isn't much to do in Requa, but if you were looking for night life, fancy restaurants and tourist attractions, you'd have stayed in San Francisco.

I think this Inn is a deal, but if you'd rather camp or RV, drive down Mouth of Klamath, and at the end you'll drive into Requa Resort. The Requa Resort is a full-service campground located just above the Klamath River's confluence with the ocean. The Resort boasts beautiful views of one the California's most pristine estuaries. There are ample opportunities for fishing, hiking, birding or just enjoying an uncrowded beach, during the

summer months. The resort is fully equipped with full RV hookups for power and sewage, picnic tables, barbeque pits, hot showers, a convenience store and more. The resort is open from May 1 to Aug. 31

The Yurok couple who manage it are friendly folks and are anxious to make it successful. Interestingly, the manager told me he went to high school in Los Gatos, and I assumed he moved here after spending his youth in a more social environment. He seems really happy getting back to the land.

There's a large parking lot, a launch ramp, a path along the bluff to the mouth and RVs pay $30 per night, $20 for tents. I like the people and the location. I would stay there and will next time I'm in the area.

Remember as you drive around and through the Klamath area, this is salmon country. You'll see the signs for salmon jerky and smoked salmon. It also clues you in, if you are a fisherman, that this is where you put your boat in the water or cast from the bank and catch salmon. They've almost disappeared from rivers and streams further south, and it's been a battle to save them here. So grab yourself some fresh "pink gold."

You've had a peaceful night's sleep and have cooked the fish you caught or have exhausted yourself kayaking and fishing, and now you are heading toward Crescent City. On your right is the **Trees of Mystery.** Why they are a mystery is a mystery to me.

It's an attractive roadside attraction, but an attraction, none the less, and I generally don't stop for those. They do have a gondola that runs through the trees. It's $14, less for kids and seniors, and they also have a motel. It's interesting to see from the road, but I can't tell more. You can get more info at: http://www.treesofmystery.net/

Now, you can almost taste the no sales tax and inexpensive gas of Oregon, as you make your way the last 16 miles to Crescent City. The next beach you come across is **False Klamath Cove**. It's a good beach for sand fans and even at times, surf lovers, and it's the last you can drive to until you approach Crescent City. Also, if the day

is calm enough, you can launch a kayak from the north end of the beach and explore places you can't see from the road. But, just before reaching the beach, look to the left for Lagoon Pond, lush, green and wet. There's a parking area, and a scenic one plus mile loop along the pond and coastal bluffs, with access to Hidden Beach.. You can also access a section of the coastal trail, taking you almost to the Klamath overlook, four miles south.

Then you climb and pull away from the coast and enter Del Norte Coast Redwoods State Park. There is only one trailhead on the ocean side, leading you to the the Damnation Creek Trail and the Coastal Trail, giving you access to coastal views between Crescent City and False Klamath Cove. The other end of this six mile stretch of Coastal Trail is at the end of Enders Rd., south of Crescent City. One mile will take you to Enders Beach, a walk in campground and the lush Nickel Creek Trail. If you want to take time to explore, look for the road heading away from the coast, and you'll see a sign for Mill Creek Campground, quieter and less crowded than the more famous Jedediah Smith park. This is a temperate rain forest, damp and thick, green and fecund. Since it is a state park, half the spaces can be reserved, the rest are first come, first served. However, as I discovered by talking to Jim at the visitors bureau, you can usually find space at either park if you get there early in the afternoon. As an additional plus, both parks, along with Gold

Bluffs Beach and Prairie Creek, further south, have a reciprocal deal with the feds, so they honor the Golden Age pass, giving you half off on camping.

As you approach Crescent City, there's a long stretch of beach before you reach the town and harbor. The first motel along that beach area is the Crescent Beach Motel, a pleasant looking place that's gotten some very good reviews. Then there's the Anchor Beach Inn    at around 100 bucks, which also has good reviews. The Curly Redwood Lodge is next and also a good place to stop. Then there's the Best Western, Lighthouse Inn and Quality Inn. But if you want to be down near the water and the historic lighthouse. I doubt if any of these places will disappoint, and you can book any of them on the internet in advance. Also, further up in Smith River there's a casino, the Lucky 7, right on the highway, and they've just added a lodge with modern, spacious rooms.

Most of what's in Crescent City is along the 101, in the business district (3rd and I) or near the harbor. The interior of town has some local shops, such as Jefferson State, a bookstore worth visiting, at 299 I Street.

Remember how Highway 101 was split into two one-way roads in downtown Eureka? Well, it's the same in Crescent City. For the traveler who doesn't want to roam, the Good Harvest is a great place for breakfast, lunch or dinner. There's also a movie theater on 101.

If you drive down Front Street, you access the harbor area, the Crescent City-Del Norte County Chamber of Commerce, cultural center and visitors bureau and the Northcoast Marine Mammal Center on

Howe. It will also take you out to the **Battery Point Lighthouse**, which has tours. It's probably one of the more visually interesting lighthouses, perched as it is on the rocks. But note that you can

192

only walk out there at low tide, so that's when they have tours.

If you take 8th or 9th down to the beach at Pebble Beach Drive, you'll be at one of the most rock-studded, photogenic stretches of beach on the coast. Between the lighthouse and Castle Rock, somewhat over two miles, there are who knows how many rocks and sea stacks: dozens? Hundreds? What makes this even better is in the summer, the waves are usually very tiny, making it easy to paddle out and explore.

Once down to Pebble Beach Drive on 8th or 9th, turn right and there will be a little road on the left going down to a very rocky little beach. You can carry—two people for this one—a kayak over the rocks to a wave-free launch. Also, you can continue on Pebble Beach, until it drops down to the beach near Castle Rock, and you can park right along the beach, for an easy carry to the water and a launch through little waves or if you surf, catch some small play waves.

If you have enough time, paddle around all the rocks, count them and write me with the total. I'd be interested.

**Castle Rock** is a wildlife refuge and it has an interesting little local ecology on it. Paddle out to it, but do not disturb whatever precariously clings to it, and you are not allowed to land there. And north of Castle Rock is Point St. George, probably not named after Curious George. Do you love the sound of a thousand sea lions singing in "harmony?" Well, paddle out to the point and listen to the concert. However, don't plan to interact with people for at least two hours, until your hearing returns. It's a memorable experience, one I recommend, as this is an incredible place for anyone who enjoys being out on the water.

Where North Pebble Beach meets Washington Blvd., you essentially leave the town and enter the point. There's parking out at the end of the road and historic buildings and some great walking paths at the point. It's also one of those locals places, where people walk after work, stroll hand in hand, play catch with their

193

dogs. While I can't call it a must see, it is one of the better places I've stopped to take a walk. You can also walk a trail all the way to the mouth of the Smith River from here, about eleven miles of wind-whipped dunes.

Just past Crescent City the 199 branches off, eventually taking you to Grants Pass Oregon on one of the more memorable drives you can imagine, but we're coasting now, so nothing more than a few miles inland. And that brings me to Jedediah Smith State Park, arguably the best redwood park in the system, sitting along the first and best "Wild and Scenic River," the Smith. In summer, green pools, linked by cascading sections of river, steep canyons above the state park, rocks in the middle to sun on, towering redwoods on both banks, wildlife in abundance, silence and serenity, Kodak moments every few feet, perfect weather and the opportunity to experience what Smith saw early in the 19th century, and that's just a sample of what it's like to visit the Smith.

Jedediah Smith State Park is 10,000 acres on the Smith River, towering redwoods, miles of hiking trails, a wonderful, deep swimming hole and a first-class state park campground. If you need to be assured of a site on a certain day, book it. Otherwise, as I found recently, you can show up on a weekday and find plenty of spaces. However, if all else fails, I'll end this chapter with my own little secret if you simply can't get into Jedediah Smith State Park and don't want to drive back down to Mill creek. You will, however, have to hang in there to the very end.

Since you probably found a spot at Jedediah Smith and you don't want to bother cooking breakfast, drive about a mile further up the 199 to the Hiouchi Café, on the right. Their sign say "Best Breakfast in the County." While I haven't tried every place, I can assure you they are a contender.

Would you like to hike/walk several miles of almost deserted beach? I thought so. If you drive out to Point St. George Heritage Area, take Pebble Beach Drive to Radio Road to the parking lot at the end. Start hiking along the beach heading north. You can start out just north of the point and continue through Tolowa Dunes State Park, along Lake Tolowa (actually part of greater Lake Earl) past Kellogg Beach, where there's a parking lot, through more of Tolowa Dunes Park and on to the mouth of the Smith

River, over ten miles of the California Coastal Trail. There are at

least five trails that branch off for further exploration of Tolowa Dunes.

**Tolowa Dunes** is a great place to wander. There are at least 16 trails, about half on the south side of the lake and the others on the north. What's great is the variety of hikes. There are lush woods, prairies with thigh-high wildflowers, streams, sloughs, marshes and beautiful rolling dunes. As an added bonus, it's mostly flat for easy walking. The Dead Lake Trail gives a sample of this variety.

Most people miss this area, leaving Crescent City and heading either north to Oregon or east on the 199. It's a big area, so let's try to bring some order to your visit. Assuming you're starting from Crescent City, and you've visited the point and haven't walked the ten plus miles north, you're headed back up Washington Blvd. toward the 101. Turn left on Riverside Road and go a mile to the end at Dead Lake. It's a small lake, but you can launch your boat there. You can walk half way around the lake and to South Big Dune and then along Sweetwater Creek a couple miles more to the beach, or you can access the Dead Lake are from the end of Sand Hill Road, off Old Mill.

Once Back on Washington, take the left on Northcrest Drive, which becomes Lake Earl Drive. Turn left on Old Mill Road. The Lake Earl Wildlife Area Information Center is at the end, and the docent there can fill you in on the area and give you a map. Rick was on duty on my first visit and he provided a wealth of local information. There's a side road at the visitor center, Sand Hill Road, which goes about a half mile to the left to another trail head. That's the start of the 4-mile Long Trail Loop. Walk through the gate, and take the narrow trail immediately on the right and through the meadow, not the gravel road. You have two miles of meadow and forest before the trail emerges into the open at the top of the dune. Follow it to the left to the flat plain behind the fore dunes and continue to Sweetwater Creek and back inland to the parking area.

From the visitor center, you can take the short (2 mile) Cadra Point Trail through forests, secluded meadows and wetlands, with side trails to the lagoon's marshy edge. Or take the longer (4.2 mile) Cadra Loop with panoramic views of the lagoon and distant mountains, and you skirt **Lake Tolowa**.

Back on Northcrest/Lake Earl Drive, continue north to Lakeview Drive, turn left and the road ends in about a mile at the lake. There's parking and a flat beach for launching your fishing boat, kayak or canoe. It's marshy along the bank here, and you are at the eastern end of the lake, so when (not if) the wind comes up, it usually will be pushing you back toward your car. There's also a short trail along Jordan Marsh, just north of Lakeview Drive.

You may hear that there's access at the end of Buzzini Road a mile further north, but don't do it. At the end is a sign saying "Private Property." It's a lie, but the local property owners obviously don't want you there, and there's nobody around to watch your car, so I wouldn't do it.

As you continue north on Lake Earl, you'll see Lake Earl Market and Deli on the right. By now you can use a snack, cup of cheap coffee and perhaps a restroom. Stop here. It's a nice place with friendly folk, and it's the only place to stop along this road.

Now, turn left on Lower Lake Drive and go two or three miles to Kellogg Road, and turn left again. This accesses Kellogg

Beach, some environmental camps, a horse parking area and the trailhead for North Ponds. It's three miles each way from the horse parking area. Take the Marsh Trail for two-tenths of a mile to a short connector trail on the right to the Ridge Trail. It's gravel road through forested dunes to the Yontocket Cemetery. You can also access this and the 6.2-mile East Ponds Loop from the end of Pala Road by going back to Lower Lake Drive and going three miles north or from the cemetery, also along Lower Lake.

There's also another launch point near there, providing a more visually interesting paddle. From Kellogg Rd. turn left on Tell Blvd., actually barely a road, to the end. This is at the neck between big Lake Earl and small Lake Tolowa. Paddling toward the beach takes through the grasses and bulrushes, home to an assortment of migratory and local waterfowl. As you enter the shallow, grassy area, you are apt to startle geese, sending them into the air. However, as I discovered recently, get an early start. It was a sunny, windless day at 10 AM. I set out for the beach, figuring that if the wind came up it would be at my back. It did come up, suddenly and with a vengeance, but from the north, soaking me and making the paddle back more work than fun.

From Pala Road you can also access the River Trail, which takes you along Yontocket Slough to the Smith River, just a mile or two up from the mouth. There are also rest rooms, river access and fishing here.

This is a very rich environmental area, if you take the time to explore it. It abounds in wildlife, pines, marsh vegetation and solitude. As I've indicated before, it's a much underused resource, used mostly by locals, and the park people are actively encouraging more visitors. If you are patient, you might see a river otter, bobcat or eagle.

When I launched my kayak, on a summer Sunday morning, at the end of Lakeview, I was the only one on the lake. Under an overcast sky, in complete silence, I shared a calm body of water with wading birds and ducks. On my Lake Tolowa paddle, the only other people I saw were in a canoe, returning from Lake Earl. On another trip I launched at the end of Tell Rd. where the two lakes join, and I paddled to the beach dunes, through reeds, but getting a late start, I fought the wind on the way back.

If you just want to launch your kayak or fishing boat on the lower part of the Smith River, take Fred Haight Drive, off the 101, just south of the small town of Smith River, and go eight-tenths of a mile to the parking lot and ramp on the river. This is perhaps three miles up from the mouth, and the mouth area extends up to the highway, approximately six miles total, and there really isn't much of a current below the 101, so it's a great area for boating, kayaking and fishing.

Above the highway, where the Smith flows from so far back into the mountains in both California and Oregon you are more likely to encounter Bigfoot than another human, you can enjoy the first Wild and Scenic River. Imagine a mountain of emeralds and sapphires, melted and flowing through a primal forest of towering trees, boulders and gorges, so rich with wildlife and solitude and off the beaten track, that you can imagine running into Jedediah Smith's

original party as they explored the area for the first time. There are rivers and there are rivers and there is the Smith. And it's no wonder that **Jedediah Smith State Park** is so popular and crowded. Also, if you have two cars, you can toss your inflatable in the river at Jedediah Smith and float down to the highway and beyond. In summer there's a lazy current.

And now, as we near the end of our trek, I'll share my best kept secret, a place even Tom Stienstra in his California Camping, arguably the best book on camping in the Golden State ever written, has left out. Ruby Van Deventer County Park is two and a half miles from 101 on 197, with connects to the 199 four miles further east, near Jehediah Smith Park. Only eight campsites, plus a group camp and day use area, these camps rest along the river, under redwoods and are not nearly as well known as other camping spots.

I've always managed to find a site here, and at times I've actually been alone. But now the cat's out of the bag, and there will be lines to get in.

Once you pass the town of Smith River, which has little to stop for, being mostly a residential community for the local Native Americans from the Smith River Indian Reservation, 101 curves back to the coast before making a short run along the beach to the border. There's a beach community, sort of a mini Sea Ranch, and there's some potential surf spots. Also that new resort and casino is along there. However, you have one more stop. Turn left on Mouth of the Smith River Rd. and drive out to the actual mouth. Standing there in a windbreaker, even in the summer, and under a low sky, watching the river give itself up to the sea, thank whatever primitive gods inhabit the cool, green north coast that you are fortunate enough to have explored this magical area.

# Other books by Meade Fischer

*Cosmic Coastal Chronicle*:A solitary wanderer travels the west coast from Big Sur to British Columbia. searching for surf, kayaking spots, hiking trails, interesting people and some insights into the great mysteries of life. Lost in a world of peace and beauty, he both celebrates and learns the lessons of life. (non fiction)

*Shattering the Crystal Face of God*: A spiritual cynic searches for personal truth and meaning in encounters with nature and the lessons of the spontaneous. (non fiction)

*Spinning Real Life:* In this satire, an idealistic young writersets out to write about real life and gets hopelessly emeshed in it, as world-changing events unfold around him and the women in his life are always one step ahead of him. (fiction)

*Messiah Chronicles*: The Jesus story, sans the miracles.A religious reformer, with his band of followers, travels ancient Judea, preaching religious reform, which angers some segments of his society.A Roman centurian takes a liking to himand tries to protect him, while keeping the peace.

*A Grand Plan*: A young girl's seven year plan for a literary career and an obsession to marry her mentor and teacher, and her attempt to get him to share her vision.

Coming soon-- **To Sea for Myself: Reflections of a Solitary Kayaker.**

**www.baymoon.com/~eclecticpress**
**eclecticpress@baymoon.com**

Or, search for Meade Fischer on amazon.com

Made in the USA
Charleston, SC
01 August 2013